Bibliographies for Biblical Research

New Testament Series
in Twenty-One Volumes

General Editor

Watson E. Mills

Bibliographies for Biblical Research

New Testament Series

in Twenty-One Volumes

Volume XIV

Pastoral Epistles

Compiled by

Watson E. Mills

MELLEN BIBLICAL PRESS

Lewiston/Queenston/Lampeter

Library of Congress Cataloging-in-Publication Data

Bibliographies for biblical research.

Includes index.
Contents: v. 1. The Gospel of Matthew / compiled by
Watson E. Mills --   -- v. 14. Pastoral Epistles
    1. Bible. N.T.--Criticism, interpretation, etc.--
Bibliography.   I. Mills, Watson E.

Z7772.L1B4   1993 [BS2341.2]   016.2262'06   93-30864

ISBN 0-7734-2347-8 (v. 1) Matthew   ISBN 0-7734-2349-4 (v. 2) Mark
ISBN 0-7734-2385-0 (v. 3) Luke   ISBN 0-7734-2357-5 (v. 4) John
ISBN 0-7734-2432-6 (v. 5) Acts   ISBN 0-7734-2418-0 (v. 6) Romans
ISBN 0-7734-2419-9 (v. 7) 1 Corinthians ISBN 0-7734-2442-3 (v. 8) 2 Corinthians
ISBN 0-7734-2468-7 (v. 9) Galatians   ISBN 0-7734-2472-5 (v. 10) Ephesians
ISBN 0-7734-2474-1 (v. 11) Philippians ISBN 0-7734-2478-4 (v. 13) 1 & 2 Thessalonians
ISBN 0-7734-2480-6 (v. 14) Pastoral Epistles ISBN 0-7734-2438-5 (v. 21) Revelation

This is volume 14 in the continuing series
Bibliographies for Biblical Research
New Testament Series
Volume 14 ISBN 0-7734-2480-6
Series ISBN 0-7734-9345-X

A CIP catalog record for this book is available from the British Library.

The Edwin Mellen Press   The Edwin Mellen Press
Box 450   Box 67
Lewiston, New York   Queenston, Ontario
USA 14092   CANADA L0S 1L0

Edwin Mellen Press, Ltd.
Lampeter, Dyfed, Wales
UNITED KINGDOM SA48 7DY

Printed in the United States of America

Dedication

In memory of my great grandfather

James Wiley Mills

1850-1916

with great affection

Contents

Introduction to the Series

This volume is the fourteenth in a series of bibliographies on the books of the Christian Bible. The series also includes volumes on the Hebrew Bible as well as the deutero-canonicals. This ambitious series calls for some 35-40 volumes over the next 3-5 years compiled by practicing scholars from various traditions.

Each author (compiler) of these volumes is working within the general framework adopted for the series, i.e., citations are to works published within the twentieth century that make important contributions to the understanding of the text and backgrounds of the various books.

Obviously the former criterion is more easily quantifiable than the latter, and it is precisely at this point that an individual compiler makes her/his specific contribution. We are not intending to be comprehensive in the sense of definitive, but where resources are available, as many listings as possible have been included.

The arrangement for the entries, in most volumes in the series, consists of three divisions: scriptural citations; subject citations; commentaries. In some cases the first two categories may duplicate each other to some degree. Multiple citations by scriptural citation are also included where relevant.

Those who utilize these volumes are invited to assist the compilers by noting textual errors as well as obvious omissions that ought to be taken into account in subsequent printings. Perfection is nowhere more elusive than in the citation of bibliographic materials. We would welcome your assistance at this point.

When the series is completed, the entire contents of all volumes (updated) will be available on CD-ROM. This option will be available, without charge, to those who have subscribed to the casebound volumes.

We hope that these bibliographies will contribute to the discussions and research going on in the field among faculty as well as students. They should serve a significant role as reference works in both research and public libraries.

I wish to thank the staff and editors of the Edwin Mellen Press, and especially Professor Herbert Richardson, for his gracious support of this series.

Watson E. Mills, Series Editor
Mercer University
Macon GA 31211
April 2000

Preface

This Bibliography on the Pastoral Epistles provides an index to the journal articles, essays in collected works, books and monographs and commentaries published in the twentieth century through the early months of 1999. Technical works of scholarship, from many differing traditions constitute the bulk of the citations though I have included some selected works that intend to reinterpret this research to a wider audience.

I acknowledge the work of Paul-Émile Langevin, *Bibliographie biblique* (Les Presses de l'Université Laval, 1972, 1978, 1985). This work is especially useful in verifying Catholic publications particularly citations to French literature. These volumes are meticulously indexed by scriptural citation as well as subject. Building the database necessary for a work of this magnitude was a tedious and time-consuming task. I acknowledge with gratitude the funds for travel provided by Mercer University. These funds enabled me to travel to overseas libraries during the summers of 1994, 1995, and 1998. I especially acknowledge Dean Douglas Steeples and President R. Kirby Godsey.

I want to express my gratitude to the staff librarians at the following institutions: Baptist Theological Seminary (formally of Rüschlikon, Switzerland); Oxford University (Oxford, UK); Emory University (Atlanta, GA); Duke University

(Durham, NC); University of Zürich (Zürich, Switzerland); Southern Baptist Theological Seminary (Louisville, KY) and the Richmond Theological Seminary (Richmond, VA).

Watson E. Mills
Mercer University
Macon GA 31207
April 2000

Abbreviations

ABR	Australian Biblical Review (Melbourne)
Ang	Angelicum (Rome)
ATR	Anglican Theological Review (New York)
AUSS	Andrews University Seminary Studies (Berrien Springs MI)
BHH	Baptist History and Heritage (Nashville TN)
Bib	Biblica (Rome)
BibInt	Biblical Interpretation (Leiden)
BJRL	Bulletin of the John Rylands University Library (Manchester)
BSac	Bibliotheca Sacra (Dallas TX)
BT	Bible Translator (London)
BTB	Biblical Theology Bulletin (Jamaica NY)
BVC	Bible et Vie Chretienne (Paris)
BZ	Biblische Zeitschrift (Paderborn)
CBQ	Catholic Biblical Quarterly (Washington)
CEJ	Christian Education Journal (Glen Ellyn IL)
Ch	Churchman: A Journal of Anglican Theology (London)
CICR	Communio: International Catholic Review (Spokane WA)
Crux	Crux (Vancouver)
CT	Christianity Today (Washington)
Didask	Didaskalia (Lisbon)
DTT	Dansk Teologisk Tidsskrift (Cophenhagen)
EAJT	East Asia Journal of Theology (Singapore)
EGLMBS	Eastern Great Lakes and Midwest Biblical Society (Chicago)
EMQ	Evangelical Missions Quarterly (Washington)
EpRev	Epworth Review (London)
EQ	Evangelical Quarterly (London)
ERT	Evangelical Review of Theology (New Delhi)
ET	Expository Times (Edinburgh)
ETR	Etudes Théologiques et Religieuses (Montpellier)

EV	Esprit et Vie (Langres)
vT	Evangelische Theologie (Munich)
ExA	Ex Auditu (Princeton)
FilN	Filologia Neotestamentaria (Cordoba)
FM	Faith and Mission (Wake Forest NC)
FundJ	Fundamentalist Journal (Lynchburg VA)
FV	Foi et Vie (Paris)
GeistL	Geist und Leben (Würzburg)
Greg	Gregorianum (Rome)
GTJ	Grace Theological Journal (Winona Lake IN)
HBT	Horizons in Biblical Theology (Pittsburg PA)
Hokhma	Hokhma (Lausanne)
HTS	Hervormde Teologiese Studies (Pretoria)
IJT	Indian Journal of Theology (Serampore)
Int	Interpretation (Richmond VA)
ITQ	Irish Theological Quarterly (Maynooth)
JBL	Journal of Biblical Literature (Atlanta)
JCBRF	Journal of the Christian Brethren Research Fellowship (London)
JETS	Journal of the Evangelical Theological Society (Wheaton IL)
JianD	Jian Dao (Hong Kong)
JMGS	Journal of Modern Greek Studies (Baltimore)
JmosP	Journal of the Moscow Patriarchate (Moscow)
JPTh	Journal of Pentecostal Theology (Cleveland TN)
JRE	Journal of Religious Ethics (Knoxville TN)
JRelS	Journal of Religious Studies (Patiala India)
JSNT	Journal for the Study of the New Testament (Sheffield)
JSP	Journal for the Study of the Pseudepigrapha (Sheffield UK)
JTS	Journal of Theological Studies (Oxford)
K	Kairos: Zeitschrift für Religionswissenschaft und Theologie (Salzburg)
LQ	Lutheran Quarterly (Gettysburg PA)
LTP	Laval théologique et philosophique (Quebec)
LV	Lumen Vitae (Washington)
MAJT	Mid-America Journal of Theology (Orange City IA)
MidS	Mid-Stream (Indianapolis)
Miss	Missiology: An International Review (Scottsdale PA)
MS	Mission Studies (Leiden)
MSJ	The Master's Seminary Journal (Sun Valley CA)
MSR	Mélanges de Science Religieuse (Lille)
NovT	Novum Testamentum (Leiden)
NTS	New Testament Studies (Cambridge)
OS	Ostkirchliche Studien (Würzburg)
PatByzR	Patristic and Byzantine Review (Kingston NY)

Point	Point (Papua, New Guinea)
Pres	Presbyterion (St. Louis)
Protest	Protestantesimo (Rome)
PRS	Perspectives in Religious Studies (Macon GA)
PSB	Princeton Seminary Bulletin (Princeton NJ)
QR	Quarterly Review (Nashville TN)
RB	Revue biblique (Paris)
Reformatio	Reformatio: Evangelische Zeitschrift für Kultur und Politik (Zürich)
RevB	Revista Biblica (Buenos Aires)
RevExp	Review and Expositor (Louisville KY)
RevQ	Revue de Qumran (Paris)
RevRéf	Revue réformée (Saint-Germain-en-Laye)
RevSR	Revue des Sciences religieuses (Strasbourg)
RHPR	Revue d'histoire et de philosophie religieuses (Strasbourg)
RIL	Religion and Intellectual Life (Sweet Briar VA)
RivBib	Rivista Biblica (Brescia)
RQ	Restoration Quarterly (Austin TX)
RR	Reformed Review (Holland MI)
RTP	Revue de Théologie et de Philosophie (Lusanne)
SBLSP	Society of Biblical Literature Seminar Papers (Atlanta)
SBT	Studia Biblica et Theologica (Pasadena CA)
Scr	Scripture: Quarterly of the Catholic Biblical Association (Edinburgh)
ScrB	Scripture Bulletin (Strawberry Hill UK)
SEAJT	South East Asia Journal of Theology (Singapore)
Semeia	Semeia (Atlanta)
Skriflig	In die Skriflig (Potchefstroom)
SM	Studia Missionalia (Wuppertal-Barmen)
SNTU-A	Studien zum NT und seiner Umwelt
SouJT	Southwestern Journal of Theology (Fort Worth TX)
SR	Studies in Religion/Sciences religieuses (Toronto)
StTheol	Studia Theologica (Copenhagen)
StudB	Studia biblica (Berlin)
StudE	Studia evangelica (Berlin)
StudPat	Studia Patristica (Berlin)
TexteK	Texte und Kontexte: Exegetische Zeitschrift (Berlin)
TGl	Theologie und Glaube (Paderborn, Germany)
Themelios	Themelios (Leicester UK)
Theology	Theology (London)
TLZ	Theologische Literaturzeitung (Leipzig)
TQ	Theologische Quartalschift (Tübingen)
Trans	Transformation: An International Evangelical Dialogue on Mission and Ethics (Exeter)
TriJ	Trinity Journal (Deerfield IL)

TSR	Trinity Seminary Review (Columbus OH)
TT	Theology Today (Notre Dame IN)
TynB	Tyndale Bulletin (Cambridge)
TZ	Theologische Zeitschrift (Basel)
USQR	Union Seminary Quarterly Review (New York)
VC	Vigiliae Christianae (Amsterdam)
VD	Verbum Domini (Rome)
VoxE	Vox evangelica (London)
WesTJ	Wesleyan Theological Journal (Lakeville IN)
WLQ	Wisconsin Lutheran Quarterly (Mequon WI)
WTJ	Westminster Theological Journal (Philadelphia)
WW	Word and World (Saint Paul MN)
ZMiss	Zeitschrift für Mission (Basel)
ZNW	Zeitschrift für die neutestamentliche Wissenschaft (Tübingen)
ZTK	Zeitschrift für Theologie und Kirche (Tübingen)

PART ONE

Citations by Chapter and Verse

1 Timothy

1:1-2

0001   H. Stettler, *Die Christologie der Pastoralbriefe*. Tübingen: Vandenhoeck & Ruprecht, 1998.

1:1

0002   Michael R. Austin, "Salvation and the Divinity of Jesus," *ET* 96 (1985): 271-75.

1:3-11

0003   Stephen Westerholm, "The Law and the 'Just Man' (1 Timothy 1:3-11)," *StTheol* 36 (1982): 79-95.

1:3

0004   Gordon D. Fee, "Reflections on Church Order in the Pastoral Epistles, with Further Reflection on the Hermeneutics of *ad hoc* Documents," *JETS* 28 (1985): 141-51.

0005   Michael C. Griffiths, "Today's Missionary, Yesterday's Apostle," *EMQ* 21 (1985): 154-65.

1:4

0006   Benedict T. Viviano, "The Genres of Matthew 1-2: Light from 1 Timothy 1:4," *RB* 97 (1990): 31-53.

1:5

0007   Mark A. Seifrid, "Paul's Approach to the Old Testament in Romans 10:6-8," *TriJ* N.S. 6 (1985): 3-37.

1:6

0008   I. de la Potterie, " 'Mari d'une seule femme': Le sens théologique d'une formule paulinienne," in L. de Lorenzi, ed., *Paul de Tarse, apôtre de notre temps*. Rome: Abbaye de S. Paul, 1979. Pp. 619-38.

1:8-11

0009   John R. W. Stott, "Homosexual Marriage: Why Same Sex Partnerships Are Not a Christian Option," *CT* 29 (1985): 21-28.

1:8-10

0010   Randolph A. Nelson, "Homosexuality and Social Ethics," *WW* 5 (1985): 380-94.

1:9-10

0011   Abraham Smith, "The New Testament and Homosexuality," *QR* 11 (1991): 18-32.

1:10

0012   Richard B. Hays, "Relations Natural and Unnatural: A Response to J. Boswell's Exegesis of Romans 1," *JRE* 14 (1986): 184-215.

0013   David F. Wright, "Translating *arsenokoitai* (1 Corinthians 6:9; 1 Timothy 1:10)," *VC* 41 (1987): 396-98.

0014   James B. De Young, "The Source and New Testament Meaning of *arsenokoitai*, with Implications for Christian Ethics and Ministry," *MSJ* 3 (1992): 191-215.

0015   John T. Fitzgerald, "The Problem of Perjury in Greek Context: Prolegomena to an Exegesis of Matthew 5:33; 1 Timothy 1:10; and Didache 2,3," in L. Michael White and O. Larry Yarbrough, eds., *The Social World of the First Christians* (festschrift for Wayne A. Meeks). Minneapolis: Fortress Press, 1995. Pp. 156-77.

0016   Dale B. Martin, "*Arsenokoitês* and *Malakos*: Meanings and Consequences," in Robert L. Brawley, ed., *Biblical Ethics and Homosexuality: Listening to Scripture*. Louisville: Westminster/John Knox Press, 1996. Pp. 117-36.

0017   J. A. Harrill, "The Vice of Slave Dealers in Greco-Roman Society: The Use of a *Topos* in 1 Timothy 1:10," *JBL* 118 (1999): 97-122.

1:12-17

0018   B. Standaert, "Paul, exemple vivant de l'Évangile de grâce," *AsSeign* N.S. 55 (1974): 62-69.

0019   Gerhard Lohfink, "Die Vermittlung des Paulinismus zu den Pastoralbriefen," *BZ* N.S. 32 (1988): 169-88.

0020 H. Stettler, *Die Christologie der Pastoralbriefe*. Tübingen: Vandenhoeck & Ruprecht, 1998.

1:13

0021 Michael Wolter, "Paulus, der bekehrte Gottesfeind: zum Verständnis von 1 Tim 1:13," *NovT* 31 (1989): 48-66.

0022 P. G. R. de Villiers, "The Vice of Conceit in 1 Timothy: A Study in the Ethics of the New Testament within Its Graeco-Roman Context," *APB* 7 (1996): 37-67.

1:17

0023 C. C. Oke, "A Doxology not to God but Christ," *ET* 67 (1955-1956): 367-68.

1:18

0024 Michael A. G. Haykin, "The Fading Vision: The Spirit and Freedom in the Pastoral Epistles," *EQ* 57 (1985): 291-305.

0025 Jerry R. Young, "Shepherds, Lead," *GTJ* 6 (1985): 329-35.

1:19

0026 Peter Lampe, "Fremdsein als urchristlicher Lebensaspekt," *Reformatio* 34 (1985): 58-62.

2

0027 Vernon C. Grounds, "The Battle for Shalom," *CT* 30 (1986): 18-20.

2:1-8

0028 André Lemaire, "Conseils pour une liturgie authentique," *AsSeign* N.S. 56 (1974): 62-66.

0029 Geoffrey Wainwright, "Praying for Kings: The Place of Human Rulers in the Divine Plan of Salvation," *ExA* 2 (1986): 117-27.

2:1-7

0030 G. Gaide, "La prière missionnaire," *AsSeign* 98 (1967): 15-24.

0031 H. Stettler, *Die Christologie der Pastoralbriefe*. Tübingen: Vandenhoeck & Ruprecht, 1998.

2:1-5

0032 John H. P. Reumann, "How Do We Interpret 1 Timothy 2:1-5?" in H. George Anderson, et al., eds., *The One Mediator, the Saints, and Mary*. Minneapolis: Augsburg, 1992. Pp. 149-57.

2:1-4

0033 Paul R. Fink, "Advice from the Apostle Paul," *FundJ* 4 (1985): 36.

2:1-2

0034 Robert S. Alley, "Render to Jesus the Things that Are Jesus'," in R. Joseph Hoffmann and Gerald A Larue, eds., *Jesus in History and Myth*. Buffalo NY: Prometheus Books, 1986. Pp. 55-77.

2:1

0035 Frank Stagg, "The Gospel, Haustafel, and Women: Mark 1:1; Colossians 3:18-4:1," *FM* 2 (1985): 59-63.

2:2-4

0036 Jay E. Adams, "The Church and Her Rights," *FundJ* 2 (1983): 16-19.

2:2

0037 Jarl Ulrichsen, "Die sieben Häupter und die zehn Hörner zur Datierung der Offenbarung des Johannes," *StTheol* 39 (1985): 1-20.

2:3-6

0038 P. Trokhin, "Hope and Salvation in the Holy Scripture of the New Testament," *JMosP* 8 (1984): 67-73.

2:3-4

0039 Robert R. Hann, "Election, the Humanity of Jesus, and Possible Worlds," *JETS* 29 (1986): 295-305.

2:3

0040 Palémon Glorieux, "La révélation du Pére," *MSR* 42 (1985): 21-41.

2:4

0041 J. Alonso Diaz, "La salvación universal a partir de la exegesis de 1 Tim 2,4," *CuBi* 28 (1971): 350-61.

2:4-6

0042 Ronald J. Sider, "An Evangelical Vision for Public Policy," *Trans* 2 (1985): 1-9.

2:4

0043 Rolf Gögler, "Inkarnationsglaube und Bibeltheologie bei Origenes," *TQ* 165 (1985): 82-94.

0044 Lowell C. Green, "Universal Salvation according to the Lutheran Reformers," *LQ* 9 (1995): 281-300.

2:5-6

0045 A. T. Hanson, "The Mediator: 1 Timothy 2:5-6," in *Studies in the Pastoral Epistles*. London: SPCK, 1968. Pp. 56-64.

0046 Robert Javelet, "Marie, la femme médiatrice," *RevSR* 58 (1984): 162-71.

0047 Alvin L. Baker, "God-Man: The Two Natures of Christ," *FundJ* 3 (1984): 30-33.

0048 Jürgen Denker, "Identidad y mundo vivencial (Lebenswelt): en torno a Marcos 10:35-45 y Timoteo 2:5s," *RevB* 46 (1984): 159-69.

0049 Michael R. Austin, "Salvation and the Divinity of Jesus," *ET* 96 (1985): 271-75.

0050 Malcolm J. McVeigh, "The Fate of Those Who've Never Heard: It Depends," *EMQ* 21 (1985): 370-79.

2:6

0051 K. Romaniuk, *L'amour du Père et du Fils dans la solériologie de saint Paul*. Rome: Pontifical Biblical Press, 1961. Pp. 58-63.

0052 Ivan Pancovski, "Tugend: Weg zum Heil," *OS* 32 (1983): 105-16.

0053 C. Samuel Storms, "Defining the Elect: A Review Article," *JETS* 27 (1984): 205-18.

2:7

0054 Neal F. McBride and W. Creighton Marlowe, "Biblical Distinctives between the Content and Character of Teaching and Preaching," *CEJ* 1 (1981): 68-74.

2:8-3:12

0055 H. Baltensweiler, "Pastoralbriefe," in *Die Ehe im Neuen Testament: Exegetische Untersuchungen über Ehe, Ehelosigkeit und Ehescheidung*. Stuttgart: Zwingli, 1967. Pp. 236-42.

2:8-15

0056   Lyle Vander Broek, "Women and the Church: Approaching Difficult Passages," *RR* 38 (1985): 225-31.

0057   Alan Padgett, "Wealthy Women at Ephesus: 1 Timothy 2:8-15 in Social Context," *Int* 41 (1987): 19-31.

0058   Dorothy Kelley Patterson, "Why I Believe Southern Baptist Churches Should not Ordain Women," *BHH* 23 (1988): 56-62.

0059   Carol J. Westphal, "Coming Home," *RR* 42 (1989): 177-88.

0060   Gordon D. Fee, "Issues in Evangelical Hermeneutics III: The Great Watershed--Intentionality and Particularity/Eternality: 1 Timothy 2:8-15 as a Test Case," *Crux* 26 (1990): 31-37.

0061   Gordon D. Fee, "Women in Ministry: The Meaning of 1 Timothy 2:8-15 in Light of the Purpose of 1 Timothy," *CBRF Journal* 122 (1990): 11-18.

0062   Gloria Neufeld Redekop, "Let the Women Learn: 1 Timothy 2:8-15 Reconsidered," *SR* 19 (1990): 235-45.

0063   Gordon P. Hugenberger, "Women in Church Office: Hermeneutics or Exegesis? A Survey of Approaches to 1 Timothy 2:8-15," *JETS* 35 (1992): 341-60.

0064   Ronald W. Pierce, "Evangelicals and Gender Roles in the 1990s: 1 Timothy 2:8-15: A Test Case," *JETS* 36 (1993): 343-55.

0065   Stephen Moyer, "Expounding 1 Timothy 2:8-15," *VoxE* 24 (1994): 91-102.

0066   P. H. Towner, "Feminist Approaches to the New Testament: With Timothy 2:8-15 as a Test Case," *JianD* 7 (1997): 91-111.

0067   R. G. Gruenler, "The Mission-Lifestyle Setting of 1 Timothy 2:8-15," *JETS* 41 (1998): 215-38.

2:8-14

0068   Robert W. Schaibley, "Gender Considerations on the Pastoral Office: In Light of 1 Corinthians 14:33-36 and 1 Timothy 2:8-14," *Logia* 2 (1993): 48-54; 3 (1994): 45-51.

2:8

0069 Paul R. Fink, "Advice from the Apostle Paul," *FundJ* 4 (1985): 36.

0070 Everett Ferguson, "*Topos* in 1 Timothy 2:8," *RQ* 33 (1991): 64-73.

2:9-15

0071 Gordon D. Fee, "Reflections on Church Order in the Pastoral Epistles, with Further Reflection on the Hermeneutics of *ad hoc* Documents," *JETS* 28 (1985): 141-51.

0072 Sharon H. Gritz, "The Role of Women in the Church," in Paul A. Basden and David S. Dockery, eds., *The People of God: Essays on the Believers' Church*. Nashville: Broadman Press, 1991. Pp. 299-314.

0073 Harold O. J. Brown, "The New Testament against Itself: 1 Timothy 2:9-15 and the 'Breakthrough' of Galatians 3:28," in Andreas J. Köstenberger, et al., eds., *Women in the Church: A Fresh Analysis of 1 Timothy 2:9-15*. Grand Rapids: Baker Book House, 1995. Pp. 197-208.

0074 Thomas R. Schreiner, "An Interpretation of 1 Timothy 2:9-15: A Dialogue with Scholarship," in Andreas J. Köstenberger, et al., eds., *Women in the Church: A Fresh Analysis of 1 Timothy 2:9-15*. Grand Rapids: Baker Book House, 1995. Pp. 105-54.

0075 Robert W. Yarbrough, "The Hermeneutics of 1 Timothy 2:9-15," in Andreas J. Köstenberger, et al., eds., *Women in the Church: A Fresh Analysis of 1 Timothy 2:9-15*. Grand Rapids: Baker Book House, 1995. Pp. 155-96.

0076 Andreas J. Köstenberger, "The Crux of the Matter: Paul's Pastoral Pronouncements Regarding Women's Roles in 1 Timothy 2:9-15," *FM* 14 (1996): 24-48.

2:11-15

0077 Aida B. Spencer, "Eve at Ephesus," *JETS* 17 (1974): 215-22.

0078 Krijn A. van der Jagt, "Women Are Saved through Bearing Children," *BT* 39 (1988): 201-208.

0079 Paul W. Barnett, "Wives and Women's Ministry (1 Timothy 2:11-15)," *EQ* 61 (1989): 225-38.

0080 Aida B. Spencer, "God's Order Is Truth," *Brethren in Christ, History and Life* 13 (1990): 51-63.

0081 Douglas J. Moo, "What Does It Mean Not to Teach or Have Authority Over Men? 1 Timothy 2:11-15," in John Piper and Wayne A. Grudem, eds., *Recovering Biblical Manhood and Womanhood: A Response to Evangelical Feminism.* Wheaton: Crossway Books, 1991. Pp. 179-93, 495-99.

0082 Arthur Rowe, "Hermeneutics and 'Hard Passages' in the NT on the Role of Women in the Church: Issues from Recent Literature," *EpRev* 18 (1991): 82-88.

0083 Ann L. Bowman, "Women in Ministry: An Exegetical Study of 1 Timothy 2:11-15," *BSac* 149 (1992): 193-213.

0084 Steven M. Baugh, "The Apostle among the Amazons," *WTJ* 56 (1994): 153-71.

0085 Ben Wiebe, "Two Texts on Women: A Test of Interpretation," *HBT* 16 (1994): 54-85.

2:11-14

0086 Eva C. Topping, "Patriarchal Prejudice and Pride in Greek Christianity: Some Notes on Origins," *JMGS* 1 (1983): 7-17.

0087 Kevin Giles, "Response," in Alan Nichols, ed., *The Bible and Women's Ministry: An Australian Dialogue.* Canberra, Australia: Acorn Press, 1990. Pp. 65-87.

2:11-12

0088 Lewis R. Donelson, "The Structure of Ethical Argument in the Pastorals," *BTB* 18 (1988): 108-13.

2:12-15

0089 Rosemary Radford Ruether, "The Liberation of Christology from Patriarchy," *RIL* 2 (1985): 116-28.

2:12

0090 George W. Knight, "αὐθεντέω in Reference to Women in 1 Timothy 2:12," *NTS* 30 (1984): 143-57.

0091 Robert W. Allison, "Let Women Be Silent in the Churches (1 Corinthians 14:33b-36): What Did Paul Really Say, and What Did It Mean?" *JSNT* 32 (1988): 27-60.

0092 Leland E. Wilshire, "The *TLG* Computer and Further Reference to αὐθεντέω in 1 Timothy 2:12," *NTS* 34 (1988): 120-34.

0093 Andrew C. Perriman, "What Eve Did, What Women Shouldn't Do: The Meaning of *authenteo* in 1 Timothy 2:12," *TynB* 44 (1993): 129-42.

0094 Leland E. Wilshire, "1 Timothy 2:12 Revisited," *EQ* 65 (1993): 43-55.

0095 Robert L. Saucy, "Women's Prohibition to Teach Men: An Investigation into Its Meaning and Contemporary Application," *JETS* 37 (1994): 79-97.

0096 H. Scott Baldwin, "A Difficult Word: αὐθεντέω in 1 Timothy 2:12," in Andreas J. Köstenberger, et al., eds., *Women in the Church: A Fresh Analysis of 1 Timothy 2:9-15*. Grand Rapids: Baker Book House, 1995. Pp. 65-80.

0097 Andreas J. Köstenberger, "A Complex Sentence Structure in 1 Timothy 2:12," in Andreas J. Köstenberger, et al., eds., *Women in the Church: A Fresh Analysis of 1 Timothy 2:9-15*. Grand Rapids: Baker Book House, 1995. Pp. 81-103.

0098 Andreas J. Köstenberger, "Syntactical Background Studies to 1 Timothy 2:12 in the New Testament and Extrabiblical Greek Literature," in Stanley E. Porter and Donald A. Carson, eds., *Discourse Analysis and Other Topics in Biblical Greek*. Sheffield UK: JSOT Press, 1995. Pp. 156-79.

2:13-15

0099 A. T. Hanson, "Eve's Transgression: 1 Timothy 2:13-15," in *Studies in the Pastoral Epistles*. London: SPCK, 1968. Pp. 65-77.

0100 Jack Levison, "Is Eve to Blame: A Contextual Analysis of Sirach 25:24," *CBQ* 47 (1985): 617-23.

2:14-15

0101 R. Falconer, "1 Timothy 2:14,15," *JBL* 60 (1941): 375-79.

0102   J. Bauer, "Die Arbeit als Heilsdimension," *BL* 24 (1956-1957): 198-201.

2:14

0103   Gerald L. Bray, "The Fall Is a Human Reality," *ERT* 9 (1985): 334-38.

2:15

0104   S. Jebb, "Suggested Interpretation of 1 Timothy 2:15," *ET* 81 (1969-1970): 221-22.

0105   A.-M. Maqlingrey, "Note sur l'exégèse de 1 Tim. 2,15," *StudPat* 12 (1975): 334-39.

0106   Jarl Ulrichsen, "Noen bemerkninger til 1 Tim 2:15," *NTT* 84 (1983): 19-25.

0107   Curtis C. Mitchell, "Why Keep Bothering God: The Case for Persisting in Prayer," *CT* 29 (1985): 33-34.

0108   Tarsicius J. van Bavel, "Women as the Image of God in Augustine's De trinitate XII," in Adolar Zumkeller, ed., *Signum pietatis* (festschrift for Cornelius Petrus Mayer). Würzburg: Augustinus-Verlag, 1989. Pp. 267-88.

0109   David R. Kimberley, "1 Timothy 2:15: A Possible Understanding of a Difficult Text," *JETS* 35 (1992): 481-86.

0110   Stanley E. Porter, "What Does it Mean to be 'Saved by Childbirth'?" *JSNT* 49 (1993): 87-102.

0111   Jarl Ulrichsen, "Heil durch Kindergebären: zu 1 Tim 2:15 und seiner syrischen Version," *SEÅ* 58 (1993): 99-104.

3:1-17

0112   Gerald G. Small, "The Use of Spiritual Gifts in the Ministry of Oversight," *CEJ* 1 (1980): 21-34.

3:1-13

0113   Paul R. Fink, "Advice from the Apostle Paul," *FundJ* 4 (1985): 36.

3:1-7

0114 John S. Feinberg, "An Undersheperd or a Hireling," *FundJ* 2 (1983): 16-18.

0115 Max A. Chevallier, "L'unité plurielle de l'église d'après le Nouveau Testament," *RHPR* 66 (1986): 3-20.

0116 Ed Glasscock, "The Biblical Concept of Elder," *BSac* 144 (1987): 66-78.

0117 Walter F. Taylor, "1 Timothy 3:1-7: The Public Side of Ministry," *TSR* 14 (1992): 5-17.

0118 P. Wells, "Comment 'garder l'Église apostolique'?" *RevRéf* 49 (1998): 11-18.

3:1-4

0119 Edward Dobson, "An Overview; part 8," *FundJ* 5 (1986): 37-39.

3:1

0120 U. Holzmeister, "Si quis episcopatum desiderat, bonum opus desiderat," *Bib* 12 (1931): 41-69.

0121 Peter Trummer, "Einehe nach den Pastoralbriefen. Zum Verständnis der Termini μιᾶς γυναικὸς ἀνήρ und ἑνὸς ἀνδρος γυνή," *Bib* 51 (1970): 471-84.

0122 José O'Callaghan, "1 Tim 3:16: 4:1.3 en 7Q4?" *Bib* 53 (1972): 362-67.

0123 Frank Stagg, "The Gospel, Haustafel, and Women: Mark 1:1; Colossians 3:18-4:1," *FM* 2 (1985): 59-63.

0124 J. Lionel North, " 'Human Speech' in Paul and the Paulines: The Investigation and Meaning of *anthropinos o logos*," *NovT* 37 (1995): 50-67.

3:11

0125 Jennifer H. Stoefel, "Women Deacons in 1 Timothy: A Linguistic and Literary Look at 'Women Likewise . . . '," *NTS* 41 (1995): 442-57.

3:12

0126 S. Lyonnet, "Unius uxoris vir," *VD* 45 (1967): 3-10.

0127 Peter Trummer, "Einehe nach den Pastoralbriefen. Zum Verständnis der Termini μιᾶς γυναικὸς ἀνήρ und ἐνὸς ἄνδρος γυνή," *Bib* 51 (1970): 471-84.

3:14-16

0128 H. Stettler, *Die Christologie der Pastoralbriefe*. Tübingen: Vandenhoeck & Ruprecht, 1998.

3:15

0129 A. Jaubert, "L'image de la colonne," in *Studiorum Paulinorum Congressus 1961*. 2 volumes. Rome: Pontifical Biblical Press, 1963. 2:101-108.

0130 B. Gartner, *The Temple and the Community in Qumran and the New Testament*. SNTS #1. Cambridge: University Press, 1965. Pp. 66-71.

0131 A. T. Hanson, "The Foundation of Truth: 1 Timothy 3.15," in *Studies in the Pastoral Epistles*. London: SPCK, 1968. Pp. 5-20.

0132 Gordon D. Fee, "Reflections on Church Order in the Pastoral Epistles, with Further Reflection on the Hermeneutics of *ad hoc* Documents," *JETS* 28 (1985): 141-51.

0133 E. Butzer, "Die Witwen der Pastoralbriefe," *TexteK* 20 (1998): 35-52.

3:16

0134 J. Schmitt, "Une confession de foi liturgique," in *Jésus ressuscité dans la prédication apostolique*. Paris: Gabalda, 1949. Pp. 99-105.

0135 A. Descamps, "La justice triomphante du Christ," in *Les justes et la justice dans les Évangiles et le christianisme primitif hormis la doctrine proprement paulinienne*. Gembloux: Duculot, 1950. Pp. 84-89.

0136 L. Cerfaux, "L'hymne de 1 Tim. 3,16," in *Le Christ dans la théologie de saint Paul*. Paris: Cerf, 1954. Pp. 281-83.

0137 S. de Ausejo, "¿Es un himno a Cristo el prólogo de San Juan? Los himnos cristologicos de la Iglesia primitiva y el prólogo del IV Evangelio," in *La escatología individual neotestamentaria a la luz las ideas en los tiempos apostolicos*. Madrid: Liberia Científica Medinaceli, 1956. Pp. 307-96.

0138 David M. Stanley, "The 'Mystery' Identified with the Glorified Christ. 1 Timothy 3:16," in *Christ's Resurrection in Pauline Soteriology*. Rome: Pontifical Biblical Press, 1961. Pp. 236-39.

0139 W. Stenger, "Der Christushymnus in 1 Tim 3,16: Aufbau, Christologie, Sitz im Leben," *TTZ* 78 (1969): 33-48.

0140 R. H. Gundry, "The Form, Meaning and Background of the Hymn Quoted in 1 Timothy 3:16," in W. W. Gasque and R. P. Martin, eds., *Apostolic History and the Gospel* (festschrift for F. F. Bruce). Grand Rapids: Eerdmans, 1970. Pp. 203-22.

0141 Eduard Schweizer, "Lord of the Nations," *SEAJT* 13 (1972): 13-21.

0142 B. Rigaux, "1 Timothy 3:16; 1 Peter 3:18-22; Hebrews 1:3-4," in *Dieu l'a ressuscité: Exégèse et théologie biblique*. Gembloux: Duculot, 1973. Pp. 160-69.

0143 W. Stenger, "Textkritik als Schicksal," *BZ* 19 (1973): 240-47.

0144 W. Stenger, *Der Christushymnus 1 Tim 3,16. Eine strukturanalytische Untersuchung*. Regensburger Studien zur Theologie #6. Frankfurt: Peter Lang, 1977.

0145 W. Metzger, *Der Christushymnus. 1. Timotheus 3.16. Fragment einer Homologie der paulinischen Gemeinden*. Arbeiten zur Theologie #62. Stuttgart: Calwer, 1979.

0146 F. Manns, "Judeo-Christian Context of 1 Timothy 3:16," *TD* 29 (1981): 119-22.

0147 A. O'Leary, "The Mystery of our Religion," *Way* 21 (1981): 243-54.

0148 Kendell H. Easley, "The Pauline Usage of *pneumati* as a Reference to the Spirit of God," *JETS* 27 (1984): 299-313.

0149 Jerome Murphy-O'Connor, "Redactional Angels in 1 Timothy 3:16," *RB* 91 (1984): 178-87.

0150 Luis F. Ladaria, "Dispensatio en S Hilario de Poitiers," *Greg* 66 (1985): 429-55.

0151   Fika J. Janse Van Rensburg, "Die Timoteus-himne (1 Tim 3:16)," *HTS* suppl 1 (1989): 83-97.

0152   Edgar Haulotte, "Formation du corpus du Nouveau Testament: recherche d'un 'module' génératif intratextuel," in Christoph Theobald, ed., *Le canon des Ecritures: études historiques, exégétiques et systématiques.* Paris: Editions du Cerf, 1990. Pp. 255-439.

3:2-7

0153   F. Ross Kinsler, "Theology by the People," *West African Religion* 20 (1983): 17-36.

3:2-12

0154   I. de la Potterie, " 'Mari d'une seule femme': Le sens théologique d'une formule paulinienne," in L. de Lorenzi, ed., *Paul de Tarse, apôtre de notre temps.* Rome: Abbaye de S. Paul, 1979. Pp. 619-38.

3:2

0155   S. Lyonnet, "Unius uxoris vir," *VD* 45 (1967): 3-10.

3:3

0156   David L. Smith, "The Case for Clergy Divorce," *Didask* 2 (1991): 12-15.

3:6

0157   P. G. R. de Villiers, "The Vice of Conceit in 1 Timothy: A Study in the Ethics of the New Testament within Its Graeco-Roman Context," *APB* 7 (1996): 37-67.

3:8-13

0158   B. C. Wintle, "Patterns of Ministry in the Later Pauline Letters," *IJT* 32 (1983): 68-76.

0159   Carl Diemer, "Deacons and Other Endangered Species: A Look at the Biblical Office of Deacon," *FundJ* 3 (1984): 21-24.

3:8

0160   S. Philsy, "*Diakonia* of Women in the New Testament," *IJT* 32 (1983): 110-18.

4:1-5

0161   Gerald T. Sheppard, "The Use of Scripture within the Christian Ethical Debate concerning Same-Sex Oriented Persons," *USQR* 40 (1985): 13-35.

4:1-3

0162   William L. Lane, "1 Timothy 4:1-3: An Early Instance of Over-Realized Eschatology?" *NTS* 11 (1965): 164-67.

0163   Michael A. G. Haykin, "The Fading Vision: The Spirit and Freedom in the Pastoral Epistles," *EQ* 57 (1985): 291-305.

4:1

0164   José O'Callaghan, "1 Tim 3:16: 4:1.3 en 7Q4?" *Bib* 53 (1972): 362-67.

4:2

0165   Abraham J. Malherbe, "In Season and Out of Season: 2 Timothy 4:2 [eukairos akairos]," *JBL* 103 (1984): 235-43.

4:3

0166   C. Daniel, "Une mention paulinienne des Esséniens de Qumrân," *RevQ* 5 (1966): 553-67.

0167   José O'Callaghan, "1 Tim 3:16: 4:1.3 en 7Q4?" *Bib* 53 (1972): 362-67.

4:5

0168   J. Munck, "Discours d'adieu dans le Nouveau Testament et dans la littérature biblique," in *Aux sources de la tradition chrétienne* (festschrift for M. Maurice Goguel). Neuchâtel: Delachauz & Niestlé, 1950. Pp. 155-70.

4:6-16

0169   H. von Lips, *Glaube - Gemeinde - Amt. Zum Verständnis der Ordination in den Pastoralbriefen.* FRLANT #122. Göttingen: Vandenhoeck & Ruprecht, 1980.

0170   Marvin L. Reid, "An Exegesis of 1 Timothy 4:6-16," *FM* 9 (1991): 51-63.

4:7-8

0171   C. Spicq, "Gymnastique et morale," *RB* 54 (1947): 229-42.

4:10

0172 Daniel R. Mitchell, "Man on the Eve of Destruction," *FundJ* 3 (1984): 23-27.

0173 C. Samuel Storms, "Defining the Elect: A Review Article," *JETS* 27 (1984): 205-18.

0174 Steven M. Baugh, "Savior of All People: 1 Timothy 4:10 in Context," *WTJ* 54 (1992): 331-40.

0175 Mark J. Goodwin, "The Pauline Background of the Living God as Interpretive Context for 1 Timothy 4:10," *JSNT* 61 (1996): 65-85.

4:12-16

0176 Joseph M. Stowell, "The Effective Leader," in Charles H. Dyer and Roy B. Zuck, eds., *Integrity of Heart, Skillfulness of Hands: biblical and Leadership Studies* (festschrift for Donald K. Campbell. Grand Rapids: Baker Book House, 1994. Pp. 315-22.

4:12

0177 Paul R. Fink, "Advice from the Apostle Paul," *FundJ* 4 (1985): 36.

4:13-14

0178 Michael A. G. Haykin, "The Fading Vision: The Spirit and Freedom in the Pastoral Epistles," *EQ* 57 (1985): 291-305.

4:13

0179 G. M. Lee, "The Books and the Parchments: 1 Timothy 4:13," *Theology* 74 (1971): 168-69.

4:14-16

0180 Paul R. Fink, "Advice from the Apostle Paul," *FundJ* 4 (1985): 36.

4:14

0181 Otfried Hofius, "Zur Auslegungsgeschichte von presbyterion 1 Tim 4:14," *ZNW* 62 (1971): 128-29.

0182 Harold L. Wilmington, "The Servant of God and His Service for God," *FundJ* 2 (1983): 49.

0183 David F. Wright, "Ordination," *Themelios* N.S. 10 3 (1985): 5-9.

0184 Jerry R. Young, "Shepherds, Lead," *GTJ* 6 (1985): 329-35.

0185 John J. Kilgallen, "Reflections on *charisma(ta)* in the New Testament," *SM* 41 (1992): 289-323.

0186 Paul Beasley-Murray, "Ordination in the New Testament," in Paul Beasley-Murray, ed., *Anyone for Ordination? A Contribution to the Debate on Ordination.* Tunbridge Wells UK: MARC, 1993. Pp. 1-13

5:1-2

0187 C. Burini, "Les 'vieillards', 'nos parents' dans l'Église de Dieu 1 Tim 5,1-2," in *Paul de Tarse, apôtre de notre temps.* Rome: Abbaye de S. Paul, 1979. Pp. 697-720.

0188 Paul R. Fink, "Advice from the Apostle Paul," *FundJ* 4 (1985): 36.

0189 P. G. R. de Villiers, "The Vice of Conceit in 1 Timothy: A Study in the Ethics of the New Testament within Its Graeco-Roman Context," *APB* 7 (1996): 37-67.

5:3-16

0190 Francis C. Synge, "Studies in texts: 1 Timothy 5:3-161," *Theology* 68 (1965): 200-201.

0191 J. Ernst, "Die Witwenregel des ersten Timotheusbriefes, ein Brief auf die biblischen Ursprünge des weiblichen Ordenswesens?" *TGl* 59 (1969): 434-45.

0192 Jouette Bassler, "The Widow's Tale: A Fresh Look at 1 Timothy 5:3-16," *JBL* 103 (1984): 23-41.

0193 Gail Peterson Corrington, "Salvation, Celibacy, and Power: 'Divine Women' in Late Antiquity," *SBLSP* 24 (1985): 321-25.

0194 Bonnie Bowman Thurston, "The Widows as the 'Altar of God'," *SBLSP* 24 (1985): 279-89.

0195 Robert Macina, "Pour éclairer le terme: digamoi," *RevSR* 61 (1987): 54-73.

0196 David M. Scholer, "Feminist Hermeneutics and Evangelical Biblical Interpretation," *JETS* 30 (1987): 407-20.

0197 Bruce W. Winter, "Providentia for the Widows of 1 Timothy 5:3-16," *TynB* 39 (1988): 83-99.

0198 E. Butzer, "Die Witwen der Pastoralbriefe," *TexteK* 20 (1998): 35-52.

5:3

0199 P. G. Duncker, "quae vere viduae sunt (1 Tim. 5,3)," *Ang* 35 (1958): 121-38.

5:8

0200 R. Alastair Campbell, "*Kai malista oikeion*—A New Look at 1 Timothy 5:8," *NTS* 41 (1995): 157-60.

5:9

0201 Peter Trummer, "Einehe nach den Pastoralbriefen. Zum Verständnis der Termini μιᾶς γυναικὸς ἀνήρ und ἑνὸς ἀνδρὸς γυνή," *Bib* 51 (1970): 471-84.

5:10

0202 S. Philsy, "*Diakonia* of Women in the New Testament," *IJT* 32 (1983): 110-18.

0203 Allen Edgington, "Footwashing as an Ordinance," *GTJ* 6 (1985): 425-34.

5:11-15

0204 Gordon D. Fee, "Reflections on Church Order in the Pastoral Epistles, with Further Reflection on the Hermeneutics of *ad hoc* Documents," *JETS* 28 (1985): 141-51.

5:14

0205 Paul R. Fink, "Advice from the Apostle Paul," *FundJ* 4 (1985): 36.

0206 William A. Heth, "Unmarried 'for the Sake of the Kingdom' (Matthew 19:12) in the Early Church," *GTJ* 8 (1987): 55-88.

5:16

0207 S. Philsy, "*Diakonia* of Women in the New Testament," *IJT* 32 (1983): 110-18.

5:17-18

0208 Paul R. Fink, "Advice from the Apostle Paul," *FundJ* 4 (1985): 36.

5:17

0209 Gerald G. Small, "The Use of Spiritual Gifts in the Ministry of Oversight," *CEJ* 1 (1980): 21-34.

0210   Gordon D. Fee, "Reflections on Church Order in the Pastoral Epistles, with Further Reflection on the Hermeneutics of *ad hoc* Documents," *JETS* 28 (1985): 141-51.

0211   Frank Stagg, "The Gospel, Haustafel, and Women: Mark 1:1; Colossians 3:18-4:1," *FM* 2 (1985): 59-63.

0212   Elsie A. McKee, "Les anciens et l'interprétation de 1 Tim 5:17 chez Calvin: une curiosité dans l'histoire de l'exégèse," *RTP* 120 (1988): 411-17.

0213   Georg Schöllgen, "Die diple time von 1 Timothy 5:17," *ZNW* 80 (1989): 232-39.

0214   Elsie A. McKee, "Some Reflections on Relating Calvin's Exegesis and Theology," in Mark S. Burrows and Paul Rorem, eds., *Biblical Hermeneutics in Historical Perspective* (festschrift for Karlfried Froehlich). Grand Rapids: Eerdmans, 1991. Pp. 215-26.

0215   B. R. Keller, "Timothy 5:17—Did All πρεσβύτεροι Proclaim God's Word?" *WLQ* 96 (1999): 43-49

5:18

0216   A. E. Harvey, " 'The Workman is Worthy of His Hire': Fortunes of a Proverb in the Early Church," *NovT* 2 (1982): 209-21.

0217   John P. Meier, "The Inspiration of Scripture: But what Counts as Scripture?" *MidS* 38 (1999): 71-78.

5:19-23

0218   J. W. Fuller, "Of Elders and Triads in 1 Timothy 5:19-23," *NTS* 29 (1983): 258-63.

5:19-20

0219   D. A. Mappes, "The Discipline of a Sinning Elder," *BSac* 154 (1997): 333-43.

5:19

0220   Paul R. Fink, "Advice from the Apostle Paul," *FundJ* 4 (1985): 36.

5:20

0221   A. Burge Troxel, "Accountability without Bondage: Shepherd Leadership in the Biblical Church," *CEJ* 2 (1982): 39-46.

5:21

0222   H. Stettler, *Die Christologie der Pastoralbriefe*. Tübingen: Vandenhoeck & Ruprecht, 1998.

5:22

0223   N. Adler, "Die Handauflegung im NT bereits ein Bussritus? Zur Auslegung von 1 Tim 5,22," *Neutestamentliche Aufsätze* (festschrift for Josef Schmid). Regensburg: Pustet, 1963. Pp. 1-6.

0224   George D. Kilpatrick, "1 Timothy 5:22 and Tertullian *De Baptismo* 18:1," *JTS* N.S. 16 (1965): 127-28.

0225   Jerome D. Quinn, "Tertullian and 1 Timothy 5:22 on Imposing Hands," *StudPat* 21 (1987): 268-70.

5:23

0226   C. Spicq, "1 Timothée 5:23," in *L'Évangile hier et aujourd'hui* (festschrift for Franz-J. Lennhardt). Geneva: Labor et Fides, 1968. Pp. 143-50.

0227   Peter Jensen, "Faith and Healing in Christian Theology," *Point* 11 (1982): 153-59.

6:1

0228   Frank Stagg, "The Gospel, Haustafel, and Women: Mark 1:1; Colossians 3:18-4:1," *FM* 2 (1985): 59-63.

6:2-3

0229   H. Stettler, *Die Christologie der Pastoralbriefe*. Tübingen: Vandenhoeck & Ruprecht, 1998.

6:3-21

0230   Jukka Thurén, "Die Struktur der Schlussparänese 1 Tim 6:3-21," *TZ* 26 (1970): 241-53.

0231   Peter Dschulnigg, "Warnung vor Reichtum und Ermahnung der Reichen: 1 Tim 6:6-10,17-19 im Rahmen des Schlussteils 6:3-21," *BZ* N.S. 37 (1993): 60-77.

6:5-10

0232   Frederick E. Brenk, "Old Wineskins Recycled: *autarkeia* in 1 Timothy 6:5-10," *FilN* 3 (1990): 39-52.

6:3-5
0233   P. G. R. de Villiers, "The Vice of Conceit in 1 Timothy: A Study in the Ethics of the New Testament within Its Graeco-Roman Context," *APB* 7 (1996): 37-67.

6:6-10
0234   Paul R. Fink, "Advice from the Apostle Paul," *FundJ* 4 (1985): 36.
6:7
0235   M. J. J. Menklen, "*Oti* en 1 Tim 6:7," *Bib* 58 (1977): 532-41.

6:9-10
0236   Titus M. Kivunzi, "Biblical Basis for Financial Stewardship," *EAJT* 3 (1985): 24-34.

6:10
0237   Ken Smith, "The Stewardship of Money," *FundJ* 4 (1985): 31-33.

6:11-17
0238   R. C. Brand, "The Evolution of a Slogan," *ET* 89 (1978): 247-48.

6:11-16
0239   H. Obendiek, "Das gute Bekenntnis nach 1. Tim 6,11-16," *EvT* 6 (1946-1947): 234-57.

0240   Ernst Käsemann, "Das Formular einer neutestamentlichen Ordinationsparänese," *Neutestamentliche Studien für Rudolf Bultmann*. Berlin: Töpelmann, 1957. Pp. 261-68.

0241   L. Deiss, "Jusqu'à l'épiphanie de notre Seigneur Jésus Christ," *AsSeign* N.S. 57 (1971): 74-79.

0242   P. Wells, "Se garder soi-même dans la foi," *RevRéf* 50 (1999): 17-25.

6:11-14
0243   Christian Grappe, "Essai sur l'arrière-plan Pascal des récits de la dernière nuit de Jésus," *RHPR* 65 (1985): 105-25.

6:12-16
0244   R.-H. Esnault, "1 Timothy 6:12-16," *ETR* 30 (1955): 40-45.

6:12
0245   D. Wiederkehr, *Die Theologie der Berufung in den Paulusbriefen*. Freiburg: Universitätsverlag, 1963. Pp. 223-33.

0246   John G. Machen, "The Good Fight of Faith," *FundJ* 2 (1983): 34-36.

6:13-16

0247   H. Stettler, *Die Christologie der Pastoralbriefe*. Tübingen: Vandenhoeck & Ruprecht, 1998.

6:14

0248   M. McNamara, "The Revelation of the Messiah in the Targum and the Epiphaneia of Christ in St. Paul," in *The New Testament and the Palestinian Targum to the Pentateuch*. Rome: Pontifical Biblical Press, 1966. Pp. 246-52.

6:17-19

0249   Werner Bieder, "Reiche als Mitarbeiter der Befreiung?" *ZMiss* 17 (1991): 66-69.

6:17

0250   P. G. R. de Villiers, "The Vice of Conceit in 1 Timothy: A Study in the Ethics of the New Testament within Its Graeco-Roman Context," *APB* 7 (1996): 37-67.

0251   Ernst Käsemann, "Das Formular einer neutestamentlichen Ordinationsparänese," *Neutestamentliche Studien für Rudolf Bultmann*. Berlin: Töpelmann, 1957. Pp. 261-68.

6:20

0252   H. M. Köster, "Um eine neue theologische Sprache - Gedanken zu 1 Tim 6,20," in L. Scheffczyk, et al., eds., *Wahrheit und Verkündigung* (festschrift for Michael Schmaus). Munich: Schöningh, 1967. Pp. 449-73.

6:20

0253   Egbert Schlarb, "Miszelle zu 1 Tim 6:20," *ZNW* 77 (1986): 276-81.

6:20

0254   Klaus Berger, "Neutestamentliche Texte im Lichte der Weisheitsschrift aus der Geniza von Alt-Kairo," in Wolfgang Haase, ed., *Principat 26,1: Religion (vorkonstantinisches Christentum: Neues Testament*. New York: de Gruyter, 1992. Pp. 412-28.

2 Timothy

1:1-14

0255 John P. Meier, "The Inspiration of Scripture: But what Counts as Scripture?" *MidS* 38 (1999): 71-78.

1:3-2:13

0256 H. von Lips, *Glaube - Gemeinde - Amt. Zum Verständnis der Ordination in den Pastoralbriefen.* FRLANT #122. Göttingen: Vandenhoeck & Ruprecht, 1980.

1:3-12

0257 Gerhard Lohfink, "Die Vermittlung des Paulinismus zu den Pastoralbriefen," *BZ* N.S. 32 (1988): 169-88.

1:3-6

0258 Richard D. Patterson, "In Remembrance of Me," *FundJ* 4 (1985): 31.

1:4

0259 Richard D. Patterson, "Being Filled," *FundJ* 4 (1985): 65.

1:5

0260 C. Spicq, "Loïs, ta grand'maman," *RB* 84 (1977): 362-64.

1:6-14

0261 André Lemaire, "Conseils pour le ministère," *AsSeign* N.S. 58 (1974): 61-66.

1:6-8

0262 Michael A. G. Haykin, "The Fading Vision: The Spirit and Freedom in the Pastoral Epistles," *EQ* 57 (1985): 291-305.

1:6

0263 M. Bauza, "Ut resuscites gratiam Dei" in *El sacerdoco de Crito y los diversos grados de su participación en la Iglwsia*. Madrid: libería Cientifica Medinaceli, 1969. Pp. 55-66.

0264 F. A. J. MacDonald, "The Three R's," *ET* 89 (1978): 343-44.

0265 H. Booth, "Stir It up," *ET* 91 (1980): 369-70.

0266 David F. Wright, "Ordination," *Themelios* N.S. 10 (1985): 5-9.

0267 John J. Kilgallen, "Reflections on *charisma(ta)* in the New Testament," *SM* 41 (1992): 289-323.

0268 Paul Beasley-Murray, "Ordination in the New Testament," in Paul Beasley-Murray, ed., *Anyone for Ordination? A Contribution to the Debate on Ordination*. Tunbridge Wells UK: MARC, 1993. Pp. 1-13.

1:7

0269 Robert A. White, "Christian Faith, the Soviet Threat, and a Theology of the Enemy," *RR* 39 (1985): 16-23.

1:8-11

0270 David M. Stanley, "The Conception of the First 'Manifestation': 2 Timothy 1:8-11," in *Christ's Resurrection in Pauline Soteriology*. Rome: Pontifical Biblical Press, 1961. Pp. 244-47.

0271 H. Stettler, *Die Christologie der Pastoralbriefe*. Tübingen: Vandenhoeck & Ruprecht, 1998.

1:8-10

0272 M. Saillard, "Annoncer l'Évangile, c'est révéler le dessein de Dieu," *AsSeign* N.S. 15 (1973): 24-30.

0273 A. Viard, "L'Évangile du Christ, principe de vie et d'immortalité," *EV* 78 (1978): 25-26.

1:8

0274 D. R. Hall, "Fellow-Workers with the Gospel," *ET* 85 (1973-1974): 119-20.

1:9-11

0275 E. Pax, "2 Tim 1,9-11," in *Epiphaneia: Ein religionsgeschichtlicher Beitrag zur biblischen Theologie.* München: Zink, 1955. Pp. 231-35.

1:9

0276 D. Wiederkehr, *Die Theologie der Berufung in den Paulusbriefen.* Freiburg: Universitätsverlag, 1963. Pp. 233-40.

1:11

0277 J. M. Bover, "Illuminavit vitam," *Bib* 28 (1947): 136-46.

0278 Neal F. McBride and W. Creighton Marlowe, "Biblical Distinctives between the Content and Character of Teaching and Preaching," *CEJ* 1 (1981): 68-74.

1:12

0279 William Barclay, "Paul's Certainties: Our Security in God—2 Timothy 1:12," *ET* 69 (1957-1958): 324-27.

0280 A. M. Besnard, "'Je sais en qui j'ai mis ma foi," *VS* 98 (1958): 5-22.

0281 A. Sohier, "Je sais à qui j'ai donné ma foi," *BVC* 37 (1961): 75-78.

1:13-14

0282 Michael A. G. Haykin, "The Fading Vision: The Spirit and Freedom in the Pastoral Epistles," *EQ* 57 (1985): 291-305.

1:16-18

0283 H. Stettler, *Die Christologie der Pastoralbriefe.* Tübingen: Vandenhoeck & Ruprecht, 1998.

1:16-17

0284 W. D. Thomas, "New Testament Characters, 12: Onesiphorus," *ET* 96 (1985): 116-17.

1:17

0285 A. E. Wilhelm-Hooijebergh, "In 2 Timothy 1:17 the Greek and Latin Texts May Have a Different Meaning," in *StudB* 3 (1980): 435-38.

2:1-7

0286 H. Stettler, *Die Christologie der Pastoralbriefe*. Tübingen: Vandenhoeck & Ruprecht, 1998.

2:1-4

0287 Paul R. Fink, "Advice from the Apostle Paul," *FundJ* 4 (1985): 36.

2:2

0288 A. M. Javierre, "πιστοὶ ἄνθρωποι: Episcopado y sucesiòn apostolica en el Nuevo Testamento," in *Studiorum Paulinorum Congressus 1961*. 2 volumes. Rome: Pontifical Biblical Press, 1963. Pp. 109-18.

2:2

0289 Alvin Thompson, "Design for Growth," *CEJ* 2 (1982): 57-63.

2:8

0290 C. Burger, "Der Davidide in christlichen Bekenntnisformeln," in *Jesus als Davidssohn: Eine traditionsgeschichtliche Untersuchung*. FRLANT #98. Göttingen: Vandenhoeck & Ruprecht, 1970. Pp. 25-41.

0291 F. A. J. MacDonald, "From Interest to Faith," *ET* 93 (1981): 83-84.

0292 H. Stettler, *Die Christologie der Pastoralbriefe*. Tübingen: Vandenhoeck & Ruprecht, 1998.

2:8-13

0293 Jürgen Roloff, "Der Weg Jesu als Lebensnorm: ein Beitrag zur Christologie der Pastoralbriefe," in Cilliers Breytenbach and Henning Paulsen, eds., *Anfänge der Christologie* (festschrift for Ferdinand Hahn). Göttingen: Vandenhoeck & Ruprecht, 1991. Pp. 155-67.

2:8-12

0294 L. Deiss, "Souviens-toi de Jésus Christ," *AsSeign* N.S. 59 (1974): 61-66.

2:10-13

0295 H. Stettler, *Die Christologie der Pastoralbriefe*. Tübingen: Vandenhoeck & Ruprecht, 1998.

2:10

0296 George H. P. Thompson, "Ephesians 3:13 and 2 Timothy 2:10 in the Light of Colossians 1:24," *ET* 71 (1960): 187-89.

2:11-13

0297   Gerhard Lohfink, "Die Vermittlung des Paulinismus zu den Pastoralbriefen," *BZ* N.S. 32 (1988): 169-88.

2:11

0298   U. Holzmeister, "Assurmptionis Deiparae mysterium verbis S. Pauli 2 Tim. 2,1 Is explicatur," *VD* 18 (1938): 225-26.

2:12

0299   Harold L. Wilmington, "Bible Study," *FundJ* 1 (1982): 42-43.

0300   William Klassen, "The Ling as 'Living Law' with Particular Reference to Musonius Rufus," *SR* 14 (1985): 63-71.

2:13

0301   Jouette Bassler, " 'He Remains Faithful'," in Eugene H. Lovering and Jerry L. Sumney, eds., *Theology and Ethics in Paul and His Interpreters* (festschrift for Victor P. Furnish). Nashville: Abingdon Press, 1996. Pp. 173-83.

2:15-16

0302   Paul R. Fink, "Advice from the Apostle Paul," *FundJ* 4 (1985): 36.

2:15

0303   Robert A. Mattke, "Integration of Truth in John Wesley," *WesTJ* 8 (1973): 3-13.

2:17

0304   Neal F. McBride and W. Creighton Marlowe, "Biblical Distinctives between the Content and Character of Teaching and Preaching," *CEJ* 1 (1981): 68-74.

2:18

0305   F.-J. Steinmetz and F. Wulf, "Mit Christus auferstanden. Ausiegung und Méditation von 1 Kor 15,20; Eph 2,6 und 2 Tim 2,18," *GeistL* 42 (1969): 146-50.

0306   G. Sellin, " 'Die Auferstehung ist schon geschehen': Zur Spiritualisierung apokalyptischer Terminologie im Neuen Testament," *NovT* 25 (1983): 220-37.

2:19-21

0307   A. T. Hanson, "The Apostates: 2 Timothy 2:19-21," in *Studies in the Pastoral Epistles*. London: SPCK, 1968. Pp. 29-41.

2:19

0308   S. C. Martin, *Pauli Testamentum: 2 Timothy and the Last Words of Moses*. Rome: Editrice Pontificia Università Gregoriana, 1997.

2:20-21

0309   A. Penna, "In magna autem domo," in *Studiorum Paulinorum Congressus 1961*. 2 volumes. Rome: Pontifical Biblical Press, 1963. Pp. 195-15.

2:20

0310   Finbarr G. Clancy, "Augustine, His Predecessors and Contemporaries, and the Exegesis of 2 Timothy 2:20," in Elizabeth A. Livingstone, ed., *Studia patristica*. Volume 27: *Capadocian Fathers, Greek Authors after Nicaea, Augustine, Donatism, and Pelagianism*. Louvain: Peeters, 1993. Pp. 242-48.

2:22-23

0311   Paul R. Fink, "Advice from the Apostle Paul," *FundJ* 4 (1985): 36.

2:22

0312   W. Metzger, "Die νεωτερικαὶ ἐπιθυῆ ία in 2 Timothy 2:22," *TZ* 33 (1977): 129-36.

2:23-26

0313   L. H. Bunn, "2 Timothy 2:23-26," *ET* 41 (1929-1930): 235-37.

2:26

0314   J. P. Wilson, "The Translation of 2 Timothy 2:26," *ET* 49 (1937-1938): 45-46.

3:1-3

0315   John F. MacArthur, "Husbands, Love Your Wives," *FundJ* 4 (1985): 34-36.

3:5

0316   Charles Nichols, "God's Blueprint for the Church," *CEJ* 1 (1981): 29-31.

3:6-7

0317 Gordon D. Fee, "Reflections on Church Order in the Pastoral Epistles, with Further Reflection on the Hermeneutics of *ad hoc* Documents," *JETS* 28 (1985): 141-51.

3:8-9

0318 M. McNamara, "Jannes and Jambres," in *The New Testament and the Palestinian Targum to the Pentateuch*. Rome: Pontifical Biblical Press, 1966. Pp. 82-96.

0319 S. C. Martin, *Pauli Testamentum: 2 Timothy and the Last Words of Moses*. Rome: Editrice Pontificia Università Gregoriana, 1997.

3:8

0320 H. F. D. Sparks, "On the Form *Mambres* in the Latin Versions of 2 Timothy 3:8," *JTS* 40 (1939): 257-58.

0321 K. Koch, "Das Lamm, das Ägypten vernichtet, ein Fragment aus Jammes und Jambres und sein geschichtlicher Hintergrund," *ZNW* 57 (1966): 79-93.

0322 Stephen Gero, "Parerga to 'The Book of Jannes and Jambres'," *JSP* 9 (1991): 67-85.

3:10-17

0323 Ana Langerak, "Study of the Word: 2 Timothy 3:10-17—Mission in Faith," *MS* 10 (1993): 230-31.

0324 H. Stettler, *Die Christologie der Pastoralbriefe*. Tübingen: Vandenhoeck & Ruprecht, 1998.

3:14-4:5

0325 Martin Camroux, "Opening up the Word of God," *ET* 97 (1985): 51-52.

3:14-4:2

0326 Monika K. Hellwig, "Making Homilies for Our Times," *TT* 43 (1987): 561-68.

3:14-17

0327 A. T. Hanson, "Inspired Scripture: 2 Timothy 3:14-17," in *Studies in the Pastoral Epistles*. London: SPCK, 1968. Pp. 42-55.

0328   Donald E. Cook, "Scripture and Inspiration 2 Timothy 3:14-17," *FM* 1 (1984): 56-61.

0329   Giuseppe de Virgilio, "Ispirazione ed efficacia della Scrittura in 2 Tm 3:14-17," *RivBib* 38 (1990): 485-94.

0330   John P. Meier, "The Inspiration of Scripture: But what Counts as Scripture?" *MidS* 38 (1999): 71-78.

3:15-17

0331   H. Rosman, "Tolle, lege," *VD* 20 (1940): 118-20.

0332   Harold L. Wilmington, "The Supreme Authority of the Bible," *FundJ* 3 (1984): 47.

3:16-17

0333   T. P. McGonigal, " 'Every Scripture Is Inspired': An Exegesis of 2 Timothy 3:16-17," *SBT* 8 (1978): 53-64.

0334   George W. Knight, "From Hermeneutics to Practice: Scriptural Normativity and Culture, Revisited," *Pres* 12 (1986): 93-104.

3:16

0335   Harry Buis, "The Significance of 2 Timothy 3:16 and 2 Peter 1:21," *RR* 14 (1961): 43-49.

0336   R. J. A. Sheriffs, "Note on a Verse in the New English Bible," *EQ* 34 (1962): 91-95.

0337   Ed L. Miller, "Plenary Inspiration and 2 Timothy 3:16," *LQ* 17 (1965): 56-62.

0338   J. W. Roberts, "Note on the Adjective after *pas* in 2 Timothy 3:16," *ET* 76 (1965): 359.

0339   J. T. Sanders, *The New Testament Christological Hymns: Their Historical Religious Background*. SNTS #15. Cambridge: University Press, 1971. Pp. 15-17; 94-95.

0340   Martin Tetz, "Athanasius und die Einheit der Kirche: zur ökumenischen Bedeutung eines Kirchenvaters," *ZTK* 81 (1984): 196-219.

0341 Gennadij Nefyodov, "The Sacrament of Penance: Holy Scripture in the Christian's Act of Repentance," *JMosP* 6 (1985): 77-79.

0342 R. Daniel Shaw, "Ethnohistory, Strategy, and Bible Translation: The Case of Wycliffe and the Cause of World Mission," *Miss* 14 (1986): 47-54.

0343 Antonio Piñero, "Sobre el sentido de θεόπνευστος: 2 Tim 3:16," *FilN* 1 (1988): 143-53.

0344 Douglas A. Oss, "The Influence of Hermeneutical Frameworks in the Theonomy Debate," *WTJ* 51 (1989): 227-58.

4:1-8

0345 Otto Knoch, "Das Testament des Paulus nach dem zweiten Timotheusbrief," in *Die 'Testamente' des Petrus und Paulus.* Stuttgart: Katholisches Bibelwerk, 1973. Pp. 44-64.

0346 Raymond O. Zorn, " 'Preach the Word'," *MAJT* 7 (1991): 17-32.

0347 H. Stettler, *Die Christologie der Pastoralbriefe.* Tübingen: Vandenhoeck & Ruprecht, 1998.

4:2

0348 Neal F. McBride and W. Creighton Marlowe, "Biblical Distinctives between the Content and Character of Teaching and Preaching," *CEJ* 1 (1981): 68-74.

0349 Nickolas Kurtaneck, "Are Seminaries Preparing Prospective Pastors to Preach the Word of God?" *GTJ* 6 (1985): 361-71.

4:5

0350 Paul R. Fink, "Advice from the Apostle Paul," *FundJ* 4 (1985): 36.

4:6-22

0351 M. C. Bligh, "Seventeen Verses Written for Timothy," *ET* 109 (1998): 364-69.

4:6-18

0352 Pierre Dornier, "Paul au soir de sa vie," *AsSeign* N.S. 61 (1972): 60-65.

4:6-8

0353 V. C. Pfitzner, "Timothy's *gumnasia* in Godliness," in *Paul and the Agon Motif: Traditional Athletic Imagery in the Pauline Literature.* Leiden: Brill, 1 1967. Pp. 171-77.

0354 David Cook, "2 Timothy 4:6-8 and the Epistle to the Philippians," *JTS* N.S. 33 (1982): 168-71.

0355 M. Peaston, "Disengagetnent," *ET* 93 (1982): 180-82.

0356 B. P. Robinson, "Paul's Character in the Face of Death," *ScrB* 28 (1998): 77-87.

4:6-7

0357 Richard D. Patterson, "Pouring out," *FundJ* 2 (1983): 19.

4:6

0358 Harold L. Wilmington, "The Servant of God and His Service for God," *FundJ* 2 (1983): 49.

4:7-8

0359 Ivan N. Stragorodsky, "Veneration of the Mother of God in the Holy Orthodox Church," *JMosP* 9 (1983): 72-74.

4:7

0360 J. J. Twomey, "I have Fought the Good Fight," *SCR* 10 (1958): 110-15.

0361 J. M. T. Barton, "Bonum certamen certavi... fidern servavi," *Bib* 40 (1959): 878-84.

4:8

0362 A. Sohier, "Je sais à qui j'ai donné ma foi," *BVC* 37 (1961): 75-78.

4:9-21

0363 Terence Y. Mullins, "A Comparison between 2 Timothy and the Book of Acts," *AUSS* 31 (1993): 199-203.

4:9-18

0364 K. H. Schelkle, "Jesus und Paulus lesen die Bibel," *BK* 36 (1981): 277-79.

4:11

0365   Michael C. Griffths, "Today's Missionary, Yesterday's Apostle," *EMQ* 21 (1985): 154-65.

4:13

0366   Peter Trummer, "Mantel und Schriften, 2 Tim 4:13: zur Interpretation einer persönlichen Notiz in den Pastoralbriefen," *BZ* N.S. 18 (1974): 193-207.

0367   T. C. Skeat, " 'Especially the Parchments': A Note on 2 Timothy 4:13," *JTS* 30 (1979): 173-77.

0368   Karl P. Donfried, "Paul as *Skenopoios* and the Use of the Codex in Early Christianity," in Karl Kertelge, eds., *Christus bezeugen* (festschrift for Wolfgang Trilling. Leipzig: St. Benno, 1989. Pp. 249-56.

4:16-22

0369   H. Stettler, *Die Christologie der Pastoralbriefe*. Tübingen: Vandenhoeck & Ruprecht, 1998.

Titus

1:1-2

0370 David M. Stanley, "The Apostle Paul as Saint," *SM* 35 (1986): 71-97.

1:4-9

0371 B. M. Metzger, "A Hitherto Neglected Early Fragment of the Epistle to Titus," *NovT* 1 (1956): 149-50.

1:5-9

0372 Gerald G. Small, "The Use of Spiritual Gifts in the Ministry of Oversight," *CEJ* 1 (1980): 21-34.

0373 Jerry R. Young, "Shepherds, Lead," *GTJ* 6 (1985): 329-35.

0374 Max A. Chevallier, "L'unité plurielle de l'église d'après le Nouveau Testament," *RHPR* 66 (1986): 3-20.

0375 Jean François Collange, "La déroute de l'aveugle (Mc 8:22-26): Ecriture et pratique chrétienne," *RHPR* 66 (1986): 21-28.

0376 Ed Glasscock, "The Biblical Concept of Elder," *BSac* 144 (1987): 66-78.

1:6-9

0377 John S. Feinberg, "An Undersheperd or a Hireling," *FundJ* 2 (1983): 6-18.

0378 F. Ross Kinsler, "Theology by the People," *West African Religion* 20 (1983): 17-36.

1:6

0379 Peter Trummer, "Einehe nach den Pastoralbriefen: Zum Verständnis der Termini μιᾶς γυναικὸς ἀνήρ und ἑνὸς ἀνδρὸς γυνή," *Bib* 51 (1970): 471-84.

1:10-16

0380 Wolfgang Stegemann, et al., trans. David E. Orton, "Anti-semitic and Racist Prejudices in Titus 1:10-16," in Mark G. Brett, ed., *Ethnicity and the Bible*. Leiden: E. J. Brill, 1996. Pp. 271-94.

1:12-13

0381 Anthony C. Thiselton, "The Logical Role of the Liar Paradox in Titus 1:12,13: A Dissent from the Commentaries in the Light of Philosophical and Logical Analysis," *BibInt* 2 (1994): 207-23.

1:12

0382 G. Folliet, "Les citations de Actes 17,28 et Tite 1:12 chez Augustin," *REA* 11 (1965): 293-95.

0383 G. M. Lee, "Ephimenides in the Epistle to Titus," *NovT* 22 (1980): 96.

1:15

0384 Gerhard Lohfink, "Die Vermittlung des Paulinismus zu den Pastoralbriefen," *BZ* N.S. 32 (1988): 169-88.

2:1-10

0385 H. Baltensweiler, "Pastoralbriefe," in *Die Ehe im Neuen Testament: Exegetische Untersuchungen über Ehe, Ehelosigkeit und Ehescheidung*. Stuttgart: Zwingli, 1967. Pp. 236-42.

0386 Frank Stagg, "The Gospel, Haustafel, and Women: Mark 1:1; Colossians 3:18-4:1," *FM* 2 (1985): 59-63.

0387 Alan Padgett, "The Pauline Rationale for Submission: Biblical Feminism and the *Hina* Clauses of Titus 2:1-10," *EQ* 59 (1987): 39-52.

2:1-4

0388 H. Stettler, *Die Christologie der Pastoralbriefe*. Tübingen: Vandenhoeck & Ruprecht, 1998.

2:3-5
    0389   Paul R. Fink, "Advice from the Apostle Paul," *FundJ* 4 (1985): 36.

2:7-8
    0390   Jerry R. Young, "Shepherds, Lead," *GTJ* 6 (1985): 329-35.

2:10-14
    0391   S. C. Mott, "Greek Ethics and Christian Conversion: The Philonic
                Background of Titus 2:10-14 and 3:3-7," *NovT* 20 (1978): 22-48.

2:11-15
    0392   L. Deiss, "'La grâce de Dieu s'est manifestée," *AsSeign* N.S. 10
                (1970): 26-31.

    0393   U. Holzmeister, "Apparuit gratia Dei Salvatoris nostri," *VD* 11
                (1931): 353-56.

    0394   F. Ogara, "Apparuit gratia Dei Salvatoris nostri," *VD* 15 (1935):
                363-72.

    0395   K. Romaniuk, *L'amour du Père et du Fils dans la solériologie de
                saint Paul*. Rome: Pontifical Biblical Press, 1961. Pp. 58-63.

    0396   A. Sisti, "La Pedagogia di Dio," *BibO* 9 (1967): 253-62.

    0397   F. Buchholz, "Predigt über Titus 2:11-15," *EvT* 7 (1947-1948):
                257-63.

2:11-14
    0398   David M. Stanley, "The Hellenized Version of the Gospel: 2 Timothy
                2:11-14," in *Christ's Resurrection in Pauline Soteriology*. Rome:
                Pontifical Biblical Press, 1961. Pp. 239-42.

    0399   A. Viard, "La grâce de Dieu et le salut des hommes," *EV* 82 (1982):
                340-41.

    0400   H. Stettler, *Die Christologie der Pastoralbriefe*. Tübingen:
                Vandenhoeck & Ruprecht, 1998.

2:11-13
    0401   E. Pax, "Tit 2,11ff," in *Epiphaneia: Ein religionsgeschichtlicher
                Beitrag zur biblischen Theologie*. München: Zink, 1955. Pp. 238-245.

<u>2:11</u>

0402 T. Vargha, "Apparuit gratia Dei," *VD* 14 (1934): 3-6.

0403 F. Wulf, "Erschienen ist die Gnade Gottes," *GeistL* 40 (1967): 401-403.

<u>2:12</u>

0404 Klaus Bockmuehl, "To Live Soberly, Righteously, and Godly in the Present Age: A Meditation on Titus 2:12," *Crux* 21 (1985): 2-5.

<u>2:13</u>

0405 Michael R. Austin, "Salvation and the Divinity of Jesus," *ET* 96 (1985): 271-75.

<u>3:1-7</u>

0406 H. Stettler, *Die Christologie der Pastoralbriefe*. Tübingen: Vandenhoeck & Ruprecht, 1998.

<u>3:1-2</u>

0407 Geoffrey Wainwright, "Praying for Kings: The Place of Human Rulers in the Divine Plan of Salvation," *ExA* 2 (1986): 117-27.

<u>3:3-7</u>

0408 S. C. Mott, "Greek Ethics and Christian Conversion: The Philonic Background of Titus 2:10-14 and 3:3-7," *NovT* 20 (1978): 22-48.

0409 Gerhard Lohfink, "Die Vermittlung des Paulinismus zu den Pastoralbriefen," *BZ* N.S. 32 (1988): 169-88.

<u>3:4-8</u>

0410 Michael A. G. Haykin, "The Fading Vision: The Spirit and Freedom in the Pastoral Epistles," *EQ* 57 (1985): 291-305.

<u>3:4-7</u>

0411 L. Deiss, "La bonté et la 'philanthropie' de Dieu notre Sauveur," *AsSeign* N.S. 10 (1970): 32-37.

0412 T. Söding, "Gottes Menschenfreundlichkeit: Eine exegetische Meditation von Titus 3," *GeistL* 71 (1998): 410-422.

<u>3:4-5</u>

0413 W. Keuck, "Sein Erbarmen: Zum Titusbrief," *BL* 3 (1962): 279-84.

3:5-6

    0414 R. Penna, "Titus 3:5b-6," in *Lo Spirito di Cristo: Cristrologia e pneumatologia secondo un'originale formulazione paolina.* Brescia: Paideia, 1976. Pp. 288-89.

    0415 Charles L. Holman, "Titus 3.5-6: A Window on Worldwide Pentecost," *JPTh* 8 (1996): 53-62.

3:5

    0416 John S. Pobee, "Human Transformation: A Biblical View," *MS* 2 (1985): 5-9.

    0417 John F. Brug, "A Rebirth-Washing and a Renewal-Holy Spirit," *WLQ* 92 (1995): 124-28.

3:13

    0418 Walter L. Liefeld, "Can Deputation Be Defended Biblically?" *EMQ* 22 (1986): 360-65.

PART TWO

Citations by Subjects

anthropology

0419 Alan Padgett, "The Pauline Rationale for Submission: Biblical Feminism and the *Hina* Clauses of Titus 2:1-10," *EQ* 59 (1987): 39-52.

antisemiticism

0420 James D. G. Dunn, "Anti-Semitism in the Deutero-Pauline Literature," in Craig A. Evans and Donald A. Hagner, eds., *Anti-Semitism and Early Christianity: Issues of Polemic and Faith.* Minneapolis: Fortress Press, 1993. Pp. 151-65.

atonement

0421 Ivan Pancovski, "Tugend: Weg zum Heil," *OS* 32 (1983): 105-16.

0422 C. Samuel Storms, "Defining the Elect: A Review Article," *JETS* 27 (1984): 205-18.

0423 I. Howard Marshall, "Universal Grace and Atonement in the Pastoral Epistles," in Clark H. Pinnock, ed., *The Grace of God, the Will of Man: A Case of Arminianism.* Grand Rapids: Zondervan, 1989. Pp. 51-69.

baptism

0424 A. T. Hanson, "Elements of a Baptismal Liturgy in Titus," in *Studies in the Pastoral Epistles.* London: SPCK, 1968. Pp. 78-96.

0425 David F. Wright, "Ordination," *Themelios* N.S. 10 3 (1985): 5-9.

0426 Max A. Chevallier, "L'unité plurielle de l'église d'après le Nouveau Testament," *RHPR* 66 (1986): 3-20.

0427 Jerome D. Quinn, "Tertullian and 1 Timothy 5:22 on Imposing Hands," *StudPat* 21 (1987): 268-70.

chiasmus

0428 Giuseppe de Virgilio, "Ispirazione ed efficacia della Scrittura in 2 Tm 3:14-17," *RivBib* 38 (1990): 485-94.

0429 John F. Brug, "A Rebirth-Washing and a Renewal-Holy Spirit," *WLQ* 92 (1995): 124-28.

Christology

0430 Karoline Läger, *Die Christologie der Pastoralbriefe.* Münster: Lit, 1996.

0431 Andrew Y. Lau, *Manifest in Flesh: The Epiphany Christology of the Pastoral Epistles*. Tübingen: Mohr, 1996.

0432 Hans Windisch, "Zur Christologie der Pastoralbriefe," *ZNW* 34 (1935): 213-38.

0433 John A. Allan, "The 'In Christ' Formula in the Pastoral Epistles," *NTS* 10 (1963): 115-21.

0434 Rudolf Schnackenburg, "Christologie des Neuen Testamentes," in Johannes Feiner and Magnus Löhrer, eds., *Mysterium salutis, 3/1: das Christusereignis*. Einsiedeln: Benziger Verlag, 1970. Pp. 230-388.

0435 Victor Hasler, "Epiphanie und Christologie in den Pastoralbriefen," *TZ* 33 (1977): 193-209.

0436 Hejne Simonsen, "Christologische Traditionselemente in den Pastoralbriefen," in Sigfred Pedersen, *Die paulinische Literatur und Theologie*. Teologiske Studier #7. Århus: Forlaget Aros, 1980. Pp. 50-62.

0437 Gerhard Lohfink, "Paulinische Theologie in der Rezeption der Pastoralbriefe," in Karl Kertelge, ed., *Paulus in den neutestamentlichen Spaetschriften: zur Paulusrezeption im Neuen Testament*. Quaestiones Disputatae #89. Freiburg: Herder, 1981. Pp. 70-121.

0438 Alvin L. Baker, "God-Man: The Two Natures of Christ," *FundJ* 3 (1984): 30-33.

0439 Palémon Glorieux, "La révélation du Pére," *MSR* 42 (1985): 21-41.

0440 Christian Grappe, "Essai sur l'arrière-plan Pascal des récits de la dernière nuit de Jésus," *RHPR* 65 (1985): 105-25.

0441 Jacques Schlosser, "La didascalie et ses agents dans les épîtres pastorales," *RevSR* 59 (1985): 81-94.

0442 I. Howard Marshall, "The Christology of Luke-Acts and the Pastoral Epistles," in Stanley E. Porter, et al., eds., *Crossing the Boundaries: Essays in Biblical Interpretation* (festschrift for Michael D. Goulder). Leiden: E. J. Brill, 1994. Pp. 167-82.

0443 I. Howard Marshall, "The Christology of the Pastoral Epistles," *SNTU-A* 13 (1988): 157-78.

0444 Jouette Bassler, "A Plethora of Ephiphanes: Christology in the Pastoral Letters," *PSB* N.S. 17 (1996): 310-25.

0445 H. Stettler, *Die Christologie der Pastoralbriefe*. Tübingen: Vandenhoeck & Ruprecht, 1998.

church and state
0446 Jay E. Adams, "The Church and Her Rights," *FundJ* 2 (1983): 16-19.

0447 Robert S. Alley, "Render to Jesus the Things that Are Jesus'," in R. Joseph Hoffmann and Gerald A Larue, eds., *Jesus in History and Myth*. Buffalo NY: Prometheus Books, 1986. Pp. 55-77.

community
0448 Karl Löning, "Epiphanie der Menschenfreundlichkeit: Zur Rede von Gott im Kontext städtischer Offentlichkeit nach den Pastoralbriefen," in Matthias Lutz-Bachmann, ed., *Und dennoch ist von Gott zu reden* (festschrift for Herbert Vorgrimler).Freiburg: Herder, 1994. Pp. 107-24.

deacons
0449 L. L. Lancaster, "The Theology of the Diaconate," *IJT* 8 (1959): 151-55.

0450 Jerome D. Quinn, "Ordination in the Pastoral Epistles," *CICR* 8 (1981): 358-69.

0451 Jennifer H. Stoefel, "Women Deacons in 1 Timothy: A Linguistic and Literary Look at 'Women Likewise . . . '," *NTS* 41 (1995): 442-57.

deutero-Pauline
0452 Egbert Schlarb, "Miszelle zu 1 Tim 6:20," *ZNW* 77 (1986): 276-81.

0453 Gerhard Lohfink, "Die Vermittlung des Paulinismus zu den Pastoralbriefen," *BZ* N.S. 32 (1988): 169-88.

divorce
0454 Edward Dobson, "An Overview; part 8," *FundJ* 5 (1986): 37-39.

0455   David L. Smith, "The Case for Clergy Divorce," *Didask* 2 (1991):
12-15.

ecclesiology

0456   Adolf von Schlatter, *Die Kirche der Griechen im Urteil des Paulus:
eine Auslegung seiner Briefe an Timotheus und Titus.* 2nd ed.
Stuttgart: Calwer Verlag, 1958.

0457   Wayne E. Oates, "Conception of Ministry in the Pastoral Epistles,"
RevExp 56 (1959): 388-410.

0458   H. Schlier, "Die Kirche nach den Pastoralbriefen," in J. Feiner and M.
Löhrer, eds., *Mysterium Salutis: Grundriss heilsgeschichtlicher
Dogmatik.* Volume 4. *Das Heilsgeschehen in der Gemeinde.*
Einsiedeln: Benziger, 1972. Pp. 179-86.

0459   Beaumont W. Powers, "Patterns of New Testament Ministry: Elders,"
Ch 87 (1973): 166-81.

0460   Daniel C. Arichea, "The Holy Spirit and the Ordained Ministry," in
Dow Kirkpatrick, ed., *The Holy Spirit.* Nashville: Tidings, 1974. Pp.
158-86.

0461   H. Goldstein, "Das Kirchenbild der Pastoralbriefe und der
Gemeindegedanke des 2. Petrusbriefs," *Paulinische Gemeinde im
Ersten Petrusbrief.* Stuttgart: Katholische Bibelwerk, 1975. Pp.
87-103.

0462   L. Floor, "Church Order in the Pastoral Epistles," in J. H. Roberts, et
al., *Ministry in the Pauline Letters.* Pretoria: New Testament Society
of South Africa, 1976 Pp. 92-109.

0463   Kevin Condon, "Church Offices by the Time of the Pastoral Epistles,"
in Andrew H. Mayes, ed., *Church Ministry.* Dublin: Dominican
Publications, 1977. Pp. 74-94.

0464   A. Burge Troxel, "Accountability without Bondage: Shepherd
Leadership in the Biblical Church," *CEJ* 2 (1982): 39-46.

0465   David Rankin, "Tertullian's Use of the Pastoral Epistles in His
Doctrine of Ministry," *ABR* 32 (1984): 18-37.

0466   Rolf Gögler, "Inkarnationsglaube und Bibeltheologie bei Origenes,"
       TQ 165 (1985): 82-94.

0467   Ferdinand Hahn, "Grundfragen von Charisma und Amt in der
       gegenwärtigen neutestamentlichen Forschung: Fragestellungen aus
       evangelischer Sicht," in Trutz Rendtorff, ed., *Charisma und
       Institution.* Gütersloh: Verlaghaus Gerd Mohn, 1985. Pp. 335-49.

0468   Randolph A. Nelson, "Homosexuality and Social Ethics," *WW* 5
       (1985): 380-94.

0469   Max A. Chevallier, "L'unité plurielle de l'église d'après le Nouveau
       Testament," *RHPR* 66 (1986): 3-20.

0470   Elsie A. McKee, "Les anciens et l'interprétation de 1 Tim 5:17 chez
       Calvin: une curiosité dans l'histoire de l'exégèse," *RTP* 120 (1988):
       411-17.

elders
0471   A. Burge Troxel, "Accountability without Bondage: Shepherd
       Leadership in the Biblical Church," *CEJ* 2 (1982): 39-46.

0472   Ed Glasscock, "The Biblical Concept of Elder," *BSac* 144 (1987):
       66-78.

0473   Elsie A. McKee, "Les anciens et l'interprétation de 1 Tim 5:17 chez
       Calvin: une curiosité dans l'histoire de l'exégèse," *RTP* 120 (1988):
       411-17.

0474   D. A. Mappes, "The Discipline of a Sinning Elder," *BSac* 154 (1997):
       333-43.

0475   B. R. Keller, "Timothy 5:17—Did All πρεσβύτεροι Proclaim God's
       Word?" *WLQ* 96 (1999): 43-49

election
0476   Robert R. Hann, "Election, the Humanity of Jesus, and Possible
       Worlds," *JETS* 29 (1986): 295-305.

eschatology
0477   Ernst Käsemann, "Eine Apologie der urchristlichen Eschatologie,"
       ZTK 49 (1952): 272-96.

0478   William L. Lane, "1 Timothy 4:1-3: An Early Instance of Over-Realized Eschatology?" *NTS* 11 (1965): 164-67.

0479   John W. Drane, "Eschatology, Ecclesiology and Catholicity in the New Testament," *ET* 83 (1972): 180-84.

0480   Gerhard Lohfink, "Paulinische Theologie in der Rezeption der Pastoralbriefe," in Karl Kertelge, ed., *Paulus in den neutestamentlichen Spaetschriften: zur Paulusrezeption im Neuen Testament*. Quaestiones Disputatae #89. Freiburg: Herder, 1981. Pp. 70-121.

0481   Daniel R. Mitchell, "Man on the Eve of Destruction," *FundJ* 3 (1984): 23-27.

0482   Luis F. Ladaria, "Dispensatio en S Hilario de Poitiers," *Greg* 66 (1985): 429-55.

0483   Peter Lampe, "Fremdsein als urchristlicher Lebensaspekt," *Reformatio* 34 (1985): 58-62.

0484   P. H. Towner, "The Present Age in the Eschatology of the Pastoral Epistles," *NTS* 32 (1986): 427-48.

0485   P. H. Towner, "Gnosis and Realized Eschatology in Ephesus and the Corinthian Enthusiasm," *JSNT* 31 (1987): 95-124.

ethics

0486   Peter Stuhlmacher, "Christliche Verantwortung bei Paulus und seinen Schülern," *EvT* 28 (1968): 165-86.

0487   Jukka Thurén, "Die Struktur der Schlussparänese 1 Tim 6:3-21," *TZ* 26 (1970): 241-53.

0488   H.-D. Wendland, "Die Pastoralbriefe: Die Ethik des bürgerlichen Christentums," *Ethik des Neuen Testaments*. Göttingen: Vanhoeck & Ruprecht, 1970. Pp. 95-101.

0489   Günter Haufe, "Gnostische Irrlehre und ihre Abwehr in den Pastoralbriefen," in Karl W. Tröger, ed., *Gnosis und Neues Testament: Studien aus Religionswissenchaft und Theologie*. Gütersloh: Gütersloher Verlaghaus Mohn, 1973. Pp. 325-39.

0490 Neil J. McEleney, "Vice Lists of the Pastoral Epistles," *CBQ* 36 (1974): 203-19.

0491 Randolph A. Nelson, "Homosexuality and Social Ethics," *WW* 5 (1985): 380-94.

0492 Gerald T. Sheppard, "The Use of Scripture within the Christian Ethical Debate concerning Same-Sex Oriented Persons," *USQR* 40 (1985): 13-35.

0493 Ronald J. Sider, "An Evangelical Vision for Public Policy," *Trans* 2 (1985): 1-9.

0494 Richard B. Hays, "Relations Natural and Unnatural: A Response to J. Boswell's Exegesis of Romans 1," *JRE* 14 (1986): 184-215.

0495 Lewis R. Donelson, "The Structure of Ethical Argument in the Pastorals," *BTB* 18 (1988): 108-13.

0496 Alfons Weiser, "Titus 2 als Gemeindeparänese," in Helmut Merklein, ed., *Neues Testament und Ethik* (festschrift for Rudolf Schnackenburg). Freiburg: Herder, 1989. Pp. 397-414.

0497 James B. De Young, "The Source and New Testament Meaning of *arsenokoitai*, with Implications for Christian Ethics and Ministry," *MSJ* 3 (1992): 191-215.

0498 Marius Reiser, "Bürgerliches Christentum in den Pastoralbriefen?" *Bib* 74 (1993): 27-44.

0499 John J. Wainwright, "Eusebeia: Syncretism or Conservative Contextualization?" *EQ* 65 (1993): 211-24.

0500 C. K. Barrett, "Deuteropauline Ethics: Some Observations," in Eugene H. Lovering Jerry L. Sumney, eds., *Theology and Ethics in Paul and His Interpreters* (festschrift for Victor P. Furnish). Nashville: Abingdon Press, 1996. Pp. 161-72.

0501 P. G. R. de Villiers, "The Vice of Conceit in 1 Timothy: A Study in the Ethics of the New Testament within Its Graeco-Roman Context," *APB* 7 (1996): 37-67.

0502 Dale B. Martin, "*Arsenokoitês* and *Malakos*: Meanings and Consequences," in Robert L. Brawley, ed., *Biblical Ethics and Homosexuality: Listening to Scripture*. Louisville: Westminster/John Knox Press, 1996. Pp. 117-36.

faith

0503 Otto Merk, "Glaube und Tat in den pastoralbriefen," *ZNW* 66 (1975): 91-102.

0504 Jerome D. Quinn, "On the Terminology for Faith, Truth, Teaching, and the Spirit in the Pastoral Epistles: A Summary," in Paul C. Empie, et al., eds., *Teaching Authority and Infallibility in the Church: Lutherans and Catholics in Dialogue VI*. Minneapolis: Augsburg Publishing House, 1978. Pp. 232-37.

0505 Dieter Lührmann, "Gal 2:9 und die katholischen Briefe: Bemerkungen zum Kanon und zur regula fidei," *ZNW* 72 (1981): 65-87.

0506 I. Howard Marshall, "Faith and Works in the Pastoral Epistles," *SNTU-A* 9 (1984): 203-18.

0507 Otto Knoch, "Torheit, Weisheit und Besonnenheit als Grundhaltungen des Christen: eine vergleichende Studie über die Entfaltung einer paulinischen Glaubensaussage in den Schriften der Paulusschule," in Walter Baier, et al., eds., *Weisheit Gottes - Weisheit der Welt* (festschrift for Joseph Kardinal Ratzinger). 2 volumes. Sankt Ottilien: EOS Verlag, 1987. Pp. 441-51.

0508 Jouette Bassler, " 'He Remains Faithful'," in Eugene H. Lovering and Jerry L. Sumney, eds., *Theology and Ethics in Paul and His Interpreters* (festschrift for Victor P. Furnish). Nashville: Abingdon Press, 1996. Pp. 173-83.

form criticism
0509 Edgar Haulotte, "Formation du corpus du Nouveau Testament: recherche d'un 'module' génératif intratextuel," in Christoph Theobald, ed., *Le canon des Ecritures: études historiques, exégétiques et systématiques*. Paris: Editions du Cerf, 1990. Pp. 255-439.

gentiles
0510 A. Feuillet, "Le dialogue avec le monde non-chrétien dans les épîtres pastorales et l'épître aux Hébreux," *EV* 98 (1988): 125-28; 152-59.

geography

0511 Terence Y. Mullins, "A Comparison between 2 Timothy and the Book of Acts," *AUSS* 31 (1993): 199-203.

gnosticism

0512 Walter Schmithals, "The Corpus Paulinum and Gnosis," in A. H. B. Logan and A. J. M. Wedderburn, eds., *The New Testament and Gnosis* (festschrift for RobertMcL. Wilson). Edinburgh: T. & T. Clark, 1983. Pp. 107-24.

0513 Jesse Sell, "The Knowledge of the Truth," in Tito Orlandi and Frederik Wisse, eds., *Acts of the Second International Congress of Coptic Studies.* Rome: CIM, 1985. Pp. 345-53.

0514 Jean-Marie Sevrin, "Vestiges d'une tradition liturgique baptismale dans des écrits du groupe Séthien," in Tito Orlandi and Frederik Wisse, eds., *Acts of the Second International Congress of Coptic Studies.* Rome: CIM, 1985. Pp. 355-66.

0515 Egbert Schlarb, "Miszelle zu 1 Tim 6:20," *ZNW* 77 (1986): 276-81.

0516 P. H. Towner, "Gnosis and Realized Eschatology in Ephesus and the Corinthian Enthusiasm," *JSNT* 31 (1987): 95-124.

0517 David R. Kimberley, "1 Timothy 2:15: A Possible Understanding of a Difficult Text," *JETS* 35 (1992): 481-86.

grace

0518 Robert Javelet, "Marie, la femme médiatrice," *RevSR* 58 (1984): 162-71.

0519 I. Howard Marshall, "Universal Grace and Atonement in the Pastoral Epistles," in Clark H. Pinnock, ed., *The Grace of God, the Will of Man: A Case of Arminianism.* Grand Rapids: Zondervan, 1989. Pp. 51-69.

0520 Steven M. Baugh, "Savior of All People: 1 Timothy 4:10 in Context," *WTJ* 54 (1992): 331-40.

0521 I. Howard Marshall, "Salvation, Grace and Works in the Later Writings in the Pauline Corpus," *NTS* 42 (1996): 339-58.

heaven
    0522   Harold L. Wilmington, "Bible Study," *FundJ* 1 (1982): 42-43.

Hellenistic influence
    0523   Luke T. Johnson, "2 Timothy and the Polemic against False Teachers: A Re-examination," *JRelS* 6-7 (1978-1979): 1-26.

    0524   Antonio Piñero, "Sobre el sentido de θεόπνευστος: 2 Tim 3:16," *FilN* 1 (1988): 143-53.

    0525   John T. Fitzgerald, "The Problem of Perjury in Greek Context: Prolegomena to an Exegesis of Matthew 5:33; 1 Timothy 1:10; and Didache 2,3," in L. Michael White and O. Larry Yarbrough, eds., *The Social World of the First Christians* (festschrift for Wayne A. Meeks). Minneapolis: Fortress Press, 1995. Pp. 156-77.

    0526   Andreas J. Köstenberger, "Syntactical Background Studies to 1 Timothy 2:12 in the New Testament and Extrabiblical Greek Literature," in Stanley E. Porter and Donald A. Carson, eds., *Discourse Analysis and Other Topics in Biblical Greek.* Sheffield UK: JSOT Press, 1995. Pp. 156-79.

heresy
    0527   J. Massyngberde Ford, "A Note on Proto-Montanism in the Pastoral Epistles," *NTS* 17 (1971): 338-46.

    0528   Lorin Cranford, "Encountering Heresy: Insight from the Pastoral Epistles," *SouJT* 22 (1980): 23-40.

    0529   Abraham J. Malherbe, "Medical Imagery in the Pastoral Epistles," in W. Eugene March, ed., *Texts and Testaments: Critical Essays on the Bible and Early Church Fathers* (festschrift for Stuart D. Currie). San Antonio: Trinity University Press, 1980. Pp. 19-35.

    0530   Walter Schmithals, "The Corpus Paulinum and Gnosis," in A. H. B. Logan and A. J. M. Wedderburn, eds., *The New Testament and Gnosis* (festschrift for Robert McL. Wilson). Edinburgh: T. & T. Clark, 1983. Pp. 107-24.

    0531   B. Paul Wolfe, "Scripture in the Pastoral Epistles: Pre-Marcion Marcionism?" *PRS* 16 (1989): 5-16.

0532 Oskar Skarsaune, "Heresy and the Pastoral Epistles," *Themelios* 20 (1994): 9-14.

0533 Jean D. Dubois, "Les pastorales, la gnose et l'hérésie," *FV* 94 (1995): 41-48.

Holy Spirit
0534 Daniel C. Arichea, "The Holy Spirit and the Ordained Ministry," in Dow Kirkpatrick, ed., *The Holy Spirit.* Nashville: Tidings, 1974. Pp. 158-86.

0535 Kendell H. Easley, "The Pauline Usage of *pneumati* as a Reference to the Spirit of God," *JETS* 27 (1984): 299-313.

0536 Michael A. G. Haykin, "The Fading Vision: The Spirit and Freedom in the Pastoral Epistles," *EQ* 57 (1985): 291-305.

0537 John J. Kilgallen, "Reflections on *charisma(ta)* in the New Testament," *SM* 41 (1992): 289-323.

0538 Charles L. Holman, "Titus 3.5-6: A Window on Worldwide Pentecost," *JPTh* 8 (1996): 53-62.

homosexuality
0539 Randolph A. Nelson, "Homosexuality and Social Ethics," *WW* 5 (1985): 380-94.

0540 Gerald T. Sheppard, "The Use of Scripture within the Christian Ethical Debate concerning Same-Sex Oriented Persons," *USQR* 40 (1985): 13-35.

0541 John R. W. Stott, "Homosexual Marriage: Why Same Sex Partnerships Are Not a Christian Option," *CT* 29 (1985): 21-28.

0542 Richard B. Hays, "Relations Natural and Unnatural: A Response to J. Boswell's Exegesis of Romans 1," *JRE* 14 (1986): 184-215.

0543 David F. Wright, "Translating *arsenokoitai* (1 Corinthians 6:9; 1 Timothy 1:10)," *VC* 41 (1987): 396-98.

0544 Abraham Smith, "The New Testament and Homosexuality," *QR* 11 (1991): 18-32.

0545   James B. De Young, "The Source and New Testament Meaning of *arsenokoitai*, with Implications for Christian Ethics and Ministry,"*MSJ* 3 (1992): 191-215.

hope

0546   Daniel R. Mitchell, "Man on the Eve of Destruction," *FundJ* 3 (1984): 23-27.

0547   P. Trokhin, "Hope and Salvation in the Holy Scripture of the New Testament," *JMosP* 8 (1984): 67-73.

household codes

0548   Jack Hannah, "Ignatian's Long Recension: Relationship to Pastorals in Household Rules," *EGLMBS* 4 (1984): 153-65.

0549   Frank Stagg, "The Gospel, Haustafel, and Women: Mark 1:1; Colossians 3:18-4:1," *FM* 2 (1985): 59-63.

0550   Alfons Weiser, "Titus 2 als Gemeindeparänese," in Helmut Merklein, ed., *Neues Testament und Ethik* (festschrift for Rudolf Schnackenburg). Freiburg: Herder, 1989. Pp. 397-414.

0551   I. Howard Marshall, "Salvation, Grace and Works in the Later Writings in the Pauline Corpus," *NTS* 42 (1996): 339-58.

hymns

0552   Eva C. Topping, "Patriarchal Prejudice and Pride in Greek Christianity: Some Notes on Origins," *JMGS* 1 (1983): 7-17.

0553   Edgar Haulotte, "Formation du corpus du Nouveau Testament: recherche d'un 'module' génératif intratextuel," in Christoph Theobald, ed., *Le canon des Ecritures: études historiques, exégétiques et systématiques*. Paris: Editions du Cerf, 1990. Pp. 255-439.

inspiration

0554   Harry Buis, "The Significance of 2 Timothy 3:16 and 2 Peter 1:21," *RR* 14 (1961): 43-49.

0555   Rolf Gögler, "Inkarnationsglaube und Bibeltheologie bei Origenes," *TQ* 165 (1985): 82-94.

0556   Giuseppe de Virgilio, "Ispirazione ed efficacia della Scrittura in 2 Tm 3:14-17," *RivBib* 38 (1990): 485-94.

0557   John P. Meier, "The Inspiration of Scripture: But what Counts as Scripture?" *MidS* 38 (1999): 71-78.

introduction

0558   Hans W. Bartsch, *Die Anfänge urchristlicher Rechtsbildungen: Studien zu den Pastoralbriefen* Hamburg-Bergstedt: H. Reich, 1965.

0559   E. Earle Ellis, *Paul and His Recent Interpreters*. Grand Rapids: Eerdmans, 1961.

0560   Percy N. Harrison, *The Problem of the Pastoral Epistles*. London: Oxford University Press, 1921.

0561   Hans H. Mayer, *Über die Pastoralbriefe* Göttingen: Vandenhoeck & Ruprecht, 1913.

0562   Yann Redalié, *Paul après Paul: le temps le Salut, la morale selon les épîtres à Timothée et à Tite*. Genève: Labor et Fides, 1994.

0563   Egbert Schlarb, *Die gesunde Lehre: Häresie und Wahrheit im Spiegel der Pastoralbriefe*. Marburg: Elwert Verlag, 1990.

0564   Alfons Weiser, *Die gesellschaftliche Verantwortung der Christen nach den Pastoralbriefen* Stuttgart: Kohlhammer, 1994.

0565   Frances Young, *The Theology of the Pastoral Letters*. Cambridge: University Press, 1994.

0566   C. Bruston, "De la date de la première épître de Paul à Timothée," *ETR* 5 (1930): 272-76.

0567   J. Johnston, "The Message of the Epistles: The Pastoral Epistles," *ET* 45 (1933-1934): 270-74.

0568   K. Pieper, "Paulus und sein junger Vikar," *TGl* 27 (1935): 617-19.

0569   P. Carrington, "The Problem of the Pastoral Epistles," *ATR* 21 (1939): 32-39.

0570   Percy N. Harrison, "Important Hypotheses Reconsidered. Part 3: Authorship of the Pastoral Letters," *ET* 67 (1955): 77-81.

0571   Laurence F. Kinney, "Pastoral Epistles," *Int* 9 (1955): 429-35.

0572   Percy N. Harrison, "The Authorship of the Pastoral Epistles," *ET* 67 (1955-1956): 77-81.

0573   Percy N. Harrison, "The Pastoral Epistles and Duncan's Ephesian Theory," *NTS* 2 (1956): 250-61.

0574   K. Grayston and G. Herdan, "Authorship of the Pastorals in the Light of Statistical Linguistics," *NTS* 6 (1959): 1-15.

0575   Curtis Vaughan, "Selected Bibliography for the Study of the Pastoral Epistles," *SouJT* 2 (1959): 7-18.

0576   B. M. Metzger, "A Reconsideration of Certain Arguments Against the Pauline Authorship of the Pastoral Epistles," *ET* 70 (1959-1960): 91-94.

0577   E. Earle Ellis, "Authorship of the Pastorals: A Résumé and Assessment of Current Trends," *EQ* 32 (1960): 151-61.

0578   Max Warren, "Commentaries on the Pastoral Epistles," *Theology* 63 (1960): 15-19.

0579   K. Wegenast, "Das Traditionsdenken der Pastoralbriefe," in *Das Verständnis der Tradition bei Paulus und in den Deuteropauhnen.* WMANT #8. Neukirchen-Vluyn: Neukirchener Verlag, 1962. Pp. 132-57.

0580   Hans von Campenhausen, "Polykarp von Smyrna und die Pastoralbriefe; and Bearbeitungen und Interpolationen des Polykarpmartyriums," in Hans F. von Campenhausen, *Aus der Frühzeit des Christentums.* Tübingen: Mohr, 1963. Pp. 197-301.

0581   Ralph G. Turnbull, *Letters to Christian Leaders.* Grand Rapids: Baker Book House, 1964.

0582   J. Rohde, "Pastoralbriefe und Acta Pauli," *StudE* 5 (1965): 303-10.

0583   Hermann Binder, "Die historische Situation der Pastoralbriefe," in Franklin C. Fry, ed., *Geschichtswirklichkeit und Glaubensbewährung* (festschrift for Friedrich Müller). Stuttgart: Evangelisches Verlagswerk, 1967. Pp. 70-83.

0584   P. Gutierrez, "Fils, disciples, successeurs," in *La paternité spirituelle selon saint Paul*. Paris: Gabalda, 1968. Pp. 225-31.

0585   Norbert Brox, "Historische und theologische Probleme der Pastoralbriefe des Neuen Testaments: Zur Dokumentation der frühchristlichen Amtsgeschichte," *K* 11 (1969): 81-94.

0586   Norbert Brox, "Zu den persönlichen Notizen der Pastoralbriefe," *BZ* N.S. 13 (1969): 76-94.

0587   Bent Noack, "Pastoralbrevenes 'troväridge tale'," *DTT* 32 (1969): 1-22.

0588   Friedrich A. Strobel, "Schreiben des Lukas? Zum sprachlichen Problem der Pastoralbriefe," *NTS* 15 (1969): 191-210.

0589   Harald Hegermann, "Der geschichtliche Ort der Pastoralbriefe," in Joachim Rogge and Gottfried Schille, eds., *Theologische Versuche 2*. Berlin: Evangelische Verlagsanstalt, 1970. Pp. 47-64.

0590   Norbert Brox, "Lukas als Verfasser der Pastoralbriefe?" in Hans J. Horn, et al., *Jahrbuch für Antike und Christentum, Jg 13*. Münster: Verlag Aschendorff, 1971. Pp. 62-77.

0591   Robert J. Karris, "Background and Significance of the Polemic of the Pastoral Epistles," *JBL* 92 (1973): 549-64.

0592   John J. O'Rourke, "Some Considerations about Attempts at Statistical Analysis of the Pauline Corpus," *CBQ* 35 (1973): 483-90.

0593   Pierre Dornier, "Les épîtres pastorales: Paul apôtre," in *Le ministère et les ministères selon le Nouveau Testament*. Paris: Seuil, 1974. Pp. 93-102.

0594   Pierre Dornier, "Paul Apôtre," in Jean Delorme, ed., *Le ministère et les ministères selon le Nouveau Testament: dossier exégétique et réflexion théologique*. Paris: éditions du Seuil, 1974. Pp. 93-102.

0595   Martin Kruse, "Seelsorge und Kirchenleitung: zur Bedeutung des
Briefes in der Kirchengeschichte," in Meinold Krauss and Joahnnes
Lundbeck, eds., *Die vielen Namen Gottes*. Stuttgart: J. F. Steinkopf
Verlag, 1974. Pp. 182-86.

0596   Pierre Le Fort, "La responsabilité politique de l'Eglise d'après les
épitres pastorales," *ETR* 49 (1974): 1-14.

0597   André Lemaire, "Les ministères dans l'Eglise," in Jean Delorme, ed.,
*Le ministère et les ministères selon le Nouveau Testament: dossier
exégétique et réflexion théologique*. Paris: éditions du Seuil, 1974. Pp.
102-17.

0598   W. Stenger, "Timotheus und Titus als literarische Gestalten," *K* 16
(1974): 252-67.

0599   R. F. Collins, "The Image of Paul in the Pastorals," *LTP* 31 (1975):
147-73.

0600   G. H. A. Kruis, "De pastoraalbrieven: ambt en macht," in A. F. M.
Engels, et al., *Wat hier gebeurt is macht: een actueel-theologisch
onderzoek - het Utrechts theologencollectief*. Hilversum: Gooi en
Sticht, 1975. Pp. 111-23.

0601   S. de Lestapis, *L'énigme des Pastorales de saint Paul*. Paris: Gabalda,
1976.

0602   S. Dockx, "Essai de chronologie de la vie de Timothée," in
Chronologies néotestamentaires et Vie de l'Église primitive (1976),
Pp. 167-78.

0603   K. Junack, "Ein Fragmentensammlung mit Teilen aus 1 Tim (0241),"
in J. K. Elliott, ed., *Studies in New Testament Language and Text*
(festschrift for George Kilpatrick). Leiden: Brill, 1976. Pp. 262-75.

0604   Bo Reicke, "Chronologie der Pastoralbriefe," *TLZ* 101 (1976): 81-94.

0605   Alexander Sand, "Anfänge einer Koordinierung verschiedener
Gemeindeordnungen nach den Pastoralbriefen," in Josef Hainz, ed.,
*Kirche im werden: Studien zum Thema Amt und Gemeinde im Neuen
Testament*. Munich: Verlag Ferdinand Schöningh, 1976. Pp. 215-37.

0606   S. G. Wilson, "The Portrait of Paul in Acts and the Pastorals," *SBLSP* 15 (1976): 397-411.

0607   Joachim Wanke, "Der verkündigte Paulus der Pastoralbriefe," in Wilhelm Ernst, et al., *Dienst der Vermittlung*. Leipzig: St Benno Verlag, 1977. Pp. 165-89.

0608   A. Feuillet, "La doctrine des Épîtres Pastorales et leurs affinités avec l'oeuvre lucanienne," *RT* 78 (1978): 181-225.

0609   Jerome D. Quinn, "The Last Volume of Luke: The Relation of Luke-Acts to the Pastoral Epistles," in Charles H. Talbert, ed., *Perspectives on Luke-Acts*. Danville VA: Association of Baptist Professors of Religion, 1978. Pp. 62-75.

0610   P. Rogers, "The Pastoral Epistles as Deutero-Pauline," *ITQ* 45 (1978): 248-60.

0611   Peter Trummer, *Die Paulustradition der Pastoralbriefe*. Beiträge zur biblischen Exegese und Theologie #8. Frankfurt: Peter Lang, 1978.

0612   Edgar Hennecke, "Apostolische Pseudepigraphen," *SNTU-A* 4 (1979): 82-89.

0613   Martin Synnes, "Paulus i pastoralbreveneal, eds.," in Ivar Asheim, et al., eds., *Israel, Kristus, kirken* (festschrift for Sverre Aalen). Oslo: Universitetsforlaget, 1979. Pp. 183-201.

0614   Josef Zmijewski, "Die Pastoralbriefe als pseudepigraphische Schriften Beschreibung, Erklärung, Bewertung," *SNTU-A* 4 (1979): 97-118.

0615   Arthur G. Patzia, "The Deutero-Pauline Hypothesis: An Attempt at Clarification," *EQ* 52 (1980): 27-42.

0616   Jerome D. Quinn, "Paul's Last Captivity," *SNTU-A* 3 (1980): 289-99.

0617   H. J. Frede, *Epistulae ad Thessalonicenses, Timotheum, Titum, Philemonem, Hebraeos*. 9. *Lieferung: 1 Tim 6,17 bis Schluss; 2 Tim 1,1-2,17*. Freiburg: Herder, 1981. Pp. 641-720.

0618   A. T. Hanson, "The Domestication of Paul: A Study in the Development of Early Christian Theology," *BJRL* 63 (1981): 402-18.

0619   Gerhard Lohfink, "Paulinische Theologie in der Rezeption der Pastoralbriefe," in Karl Kertelge, ed., *Paulus in den neutestamentlichen Spätschriften.* Freiburg: Herder, 1981. Pp. 70-121.

0620   Peter Trummer, "Corpus Paulinum - Corpus Pastorale. Zur Ortung der Paulustradition in den Pastoralbriefen," in Karl Kertelge, ed., *Paulus in den neutestamentlichen Spätschriften.* Freiburg: Herder, 1981. Pp. 122-45.

0621   J. van Bruggen, *Die geschichtliche Einordnung der Pastoralbriefe.* Theologische Verlagsgemeinschaft: Monographien und Studien Bilcher #305. Wuppertal: Brockhaus, 1981.

0622   J.-H. Churchill, "The Pastoral Epistles: A Problem for Preachers and Others," *StudE* 7 (1982): 133-40.

0623   David Cook, "2 Timothy 4:6-8 and the Epistle to the Philippians," *JTS* N.S. 33 (1982): 168-71.

0624   Georg Kretschmar, "Der paulinische Glaube in den Pastoralbriefen," in Ferdinand Hahn and Hans Klein, eds., *Glaube im Neuen Testament* (festschrift for Ehren von Hermann Binder). Neukirchen-Vluyn: Neukirchener Verlag, 1982. Pp. 115-40.

0625   Bo Reicke, "Les Pastorales dans le ministère de Paul," *Hokhma* 19 (1982): 47-61.

0626   Dennis MacDonald, *The Legend and the Apostle: The Battle for Paul in Story and Canon.* Philadelphia: Westminster, 1983.

0627   John L. White, "Saint Paul and the Apostolic Letter Tradition," *CBQ* 45 (1983): 433-44.

0628   David Cook, "The Pastoral Fragments Reconsidered," *JTS* N.S. 35 (1984): 120-31.

0629   Thomas A. Robinson, "Grayston and Herdan's 'C' Quantity Formula and the Authorship of the Pastoral Epistles," *NTS* 30 (1984): 282-88.

0630   Prosper Grech, "Timoteo e Tito: modelli del vescovo nel periodo subapostolico," in Giustino Farnedi and Philippe Rouillard, eds., *Il* *ministero ordinato nel dialogo ecumenico.* Rome: Edizioni Abbazia S Paolo, 1985. Pp. 67-75.

0631 Eduard Lohse, "Das apostolische Vermächtnis - Zum paulinischen Charakter der Pastoralbriefe," in Wolfgang Schrage, ed., *Studien zum Text und zur Ethik des Neuen Testaments* (festschrift for Heinrich Greeven). Berlin: Walter de Gruyter, 1986. Pp. 266-81.

0632 E. Earle Ellis, "Tradition in the Pastoral Letters," in C. A. Evans and W. F. Stinespring, eds., *Early Jewish and Christian Exegesis* (festschrift for William H. Brownlee). Atlanta: Scholars Press, 1987. Pp. 237-53.

0633 Peter Hofrichter, "Strukturdebatte im Namen des Apostels: zur Abhängigkeit der Pastoralbriefe untereinander und vom ersten Petrusbrief," in Norbert Brox, et al., eds., *Anfänge der Theologie: charisteion Johannes B. Bauer zum Jänner.* Graz, Austria: Styria, 1987. Pp. 101-16.

0634 Willy Rordoff, "Nochmals: Paulusakten und Pastoralbriefe," in Gerald F. Hawthorne and Otto Betz, eds., *Tradition and Interpretation in the New Testament* (festschrift for E. Earle Ellis). Grand Rapids MI: Eerdmans, 1987. Pp. 319-27.

0635 Wolfgang Schenk, "Die Briefe an Timotheus I und II und an Titus (Pastoralbriefe) in der neueren Forschung," in Wolfgang Haase, ed., *Principat 25, 4: Religion.* New York: Walter de Gruyter, 1987. Pp. 3404-38.

0636 Richard Bauckham, "Pseudo-Apostolic Letters," *JBL* 107 (1988): 469-94.

0637 Gerhard Lohfink, "Die Vermittlung des Paulinismus zu den Pastoralbriefen," *BZ* N.S. 32 (1988): 169-88.

0638 Willy Rordoff, "In welchem Verhältnis stehen die apokryphen Paulus-akten zur kanonischen Apostelgeschichte und zu den Pastoralbriefen?" in Tjitze Baarda, et al., eds., *Text and Testimony: Essays on New Testament and Apocryphal Literature* (festschrift for A. F. J. Klijn.) Kampen: Kok, 1988. Pp. 225-41.

0639 Michael Wolter, *Die Pastoralbriefe als Paulustradition.* Göttingen: Vandenhoeck & Ruprecht, 1988.

0640   John A. Ziesler, "Which is the Best Commentary? Part12: The Pastoral Epistles," *ET* 99 (1988): 264-67.

0641   J. Christiaan Beker, "The Pastoral Epistles: Paul and We," in Theodore W. Jennings, ed., *Text and Logos: The Humanistic Interpretation of the New Testament*. Atlanta: Scholars Press, 1990. Pp. 265-72.

0642   C. J. H. Venter, "Indikatief en paraklese in die verkondiging met toeligting uit die Pastorale Briewe," *Skriflig* 24 (1990): 1-26.

0643   Jerome Murphy-O'Connor, "2 Timothy Contrasted with 1 Timothy and Titus," *RB* 98 (1991): 403-18.

0644   Hermann Patsch, "Die Angst vor dem Deuteropaulinismus: die Rezeption des 'kritischen Sendschreibens' Friedrich Schleiermachers über den 1 Timotheusbrief," *ZTK* 88 (1991): 451-77.

0645   Frances Young, "The Pastoral Epistles and the Ethics of Reading," *JSNT* 45 (1992): 105-20.

0646   Daniel C. Arichea, "Authorship and Translation: The Authorship of the Pastorals and Its Implications for Translation," *BT* 44 (1993): 331-40.

0647   Richard Bauckham, "The Acts of Paul as a Sequel to Acts," in Bruce W. Winter and Andrew D. Clarke, eds., *The Book of Acts in Its First Century Setting*. Volume 1: *The Book of Acts in Its Ancient Literary Setting*. Grand Rapids: Eerdmans, 1993. Pp. 105-52.

0648   Bela B. Edwards, "The Genuineness of the Pastoral Epistle," *BSac* 150 (1993): 131-39.

0649   I. Howard Marshall, " 'Sometimes Only Orthodox'—Is There More to the Pastoral Epistles?" *EpRev* 20 (1993): 12-24.

0650   Jean D. Kaestli, "Luke-Acts and the Pastoral Epistles: the Thesis of a Common Authorship," Christopher M. Tuckett, ed., *Luke's Literary Achievement*. Sheffield: Sheffield Academic Press, 1995. in Pp. 110-26.

0651   Yann Redalié, " 'Diventa modello dei credenti': La figura pastorale nelle esortazioni a Timoteo," *Protest* 50 (1995): 2-21.

0652 P. H. Towner, "Pauline Theology or Pauline Tradition in the Pastoral Epistles: The Question of Method," *TynB* 46 (1995): 287-314.

0653 Michael D. Goulder, "The Pastor's Wolves: Jewish Christian Visionaries behind the Pastoral Epistles," *NovT* 38 (1996): 242-56.

0654 I. Howard Marshall, "Prospects for the Pastoral Epistles," in Donald M. Lewis and Alister McGrath, eds., *Doing Theology for the People of God* (festschrift for J. I. Packer). Downers Grove IL: InterVarsity Press, 1996. Pp. 137-55.

0655 James D. Miller, *The Pastoral Letters as Composite Documents*. Cambridge: University Press, 1997.

0656 H. Ponsot, "Les Pastorales seaient-elles les premières lettres de Paul," *LV* 46 (1997): 83-93.

0657 R. Reuter, *Synopse zu den Briefen des Neuen Testaments*. Volume 2. *Die Pastoralbriefe*. Frankfurt: Lang, 1998.

kenosis

0658 Peter Lampe, "Fremdsein als urchristlicher Lebensaspekt," *Reformatio* 34 (1985): 58-62.

kingdom of God

0659 Geoffrey Wainwright, "Praying for Kings: The Place of Human Rulers in the Divine Plan of Salvation," *ExA* 2 (1986): 117-27.

law

0660 William Klassen, "The Ling as 'Living Law' with Particular Reference to Musonius Rufus," *SR* 14 (1985): 63-71.

0661 Douglas A. Oss, "The Influence of Hermeneutical Frameworks in the Theonomy Debate," *WTJ* 51 (1989): 227-58.

law and gospel

0662 Stephen Westerholm, "The Law and the 'Just Man' (1 Timothy1:3-11)," *StTheol* 36 (1982): 79-95.

Lord's Supper

0663 A. T. Hanson, "Eucharistic References in 1 and 2 Timothy," in *Studies in the Pastoral Epistles*. London: SPCK, 1968. Pp. 97-109.

0664 David F. Wright, "Ordination," *Themelios* N.S. 10 3 (1985): 5-9.

0665 Max A. Chevallier, "L'unité plurielle de l'église d'après le Nouveau Testament," *RHPR* 66 (1986): 3-20.

marriage
0666 Peter Trummer, "Einehe nach den Pastoralbriefen: zum Verständnis der Termini μιᾶς γυναικὸς ἀνήρ und ἑνὸς ἀνδρὸς γυνή," *Bib* 51 (1970): 471-84.

0667 John F. MacArthur, "Husbands, Love Your Wives," *FundJ* 4 (1985): 34-36.

0668 John R. W. Stott, "Homosexual Marriage: Why Same Sex Partnerships Are Not a Christian Option," *CT* 29 (1985): 21-28.

0669 Edward Dobson, "An Overview; part 8," *FundJ* 5 (1986): 37-39.

0670 Gordon P. Hugenberger, "Women in Church Office: Hermeneutics or Exegesis? A Survey of Approaches to 1 Timothy 2:8-15," *JETS* 35 (1992): 341-60.

0671 Sydney H. T. Page, "Marital Expectations of Church Leaders in the Pastoral Epistles," *JSNT* 50 (1993): 105-20.

missions
0672 F. Ross Kinsler, "Theology by the People," *West African Religion* 20 (1983): 17-36.

0673 Malcolm J. McVeigh, "The Fate of Those Who've Never Heard: It Depends," *EMQ* 21 (1985): 370-79.

mystical body
0674 Max A. Chevallier, "L'unité plurielle de l'église d'après le Nouveau Testament," *RHPR* 66 (1986): 3-20.

paraenesis
0675 Jan L. De Villiers, "Indications of Church Rule or Government in Pauline Parenetic Material," in J. H. Roberts, et al., *Ministry in the Pauline Letters*. Pretoria: New Testament Society of South Africa, 1976 Pp. 69-80.

0676 Jürgen Roloff, "Themen und Traditionen urchristlicher Amtsträgerparänese," in Helmut Merklein, ed., *Neues Testament und Ethik* (festschrift for Rudolf Schnackenburg). Freiburg: Herder, 1989. Pp. 507-26.

0677 Alfons Weiser, "Titus 2 als Gemeindeparänese," in Helmut Merklein, ed., *Neues Testament und Ethik* (festschrift for Rudolf Schnackenburg). Freiburg: Herder, 1989. Pp. 397-414.

0678 Jerome D. Quinn, "Paraenesis and the Pastoral Epistles," *Semeia* 50 (1990) :189-210.

passion

0679 Christian Grappe, "Essai sur l'arrière-plan Pascal des récits de la dernière nuit de Jésus," *RHPR* 65 (1985): 105-25.

prayer

0680 Curtis C. Mitchell, "Why Keep Bothering God: The Case for Persisting in Prayer," *CT* 29 (1985): 33-34.

0681 Geoffrey Wainwright, "Praying for Kings: The Place of Human Rulers in the Divine Plan of Salvation," *ExA* 2 (1986): 117-27.

0682 John H. P. Reumann, "How Do We Interpret 1 Timothy 2:1-5?" in H. George Anderson, et al., eds., *The One Mediator, the Saints, and Mary*. Minneapolis: Augsburg, 1992. Pp. 149-57.

prophecy

0683 Antonio Piñero, "Sobre el sentido de θεόπνευστος: 2 Tim 3:16," *FilN* 1 (1988): 143-53.

Qumran scrolls

0684 José O'Callaghan, "1 Tim 3:16: 4:1.3 en 7Q4?" *Bib* 53 (1972): 362-67.

0685 Mark A. Seifrid, "Paul's Approach to the Old Testament in Romans 10:6-8," *TriJ* N.S. 6 (1985): 3-37.

Rabbinic literature

0686 Mark A. Seifrid, "Paul's Approach to the Old Testament in Romans 10:6-8," *TriJ* N.S. 6 (1985): 3-37.

racism

0687   Wolfgang Stegemann, et al., trans. David E. Orton, "Anti-semitic and
           Racist Prejudices in Titus 1:10-16," in Mark G. Brett, ed., *Ethnicity
           and the Bible*. Leiden: E. J. Brill, 1996. Pp. 271-94.

reconciliation
0688   Peter Stuhlmacher, "The Gospel of Reconciliation in Christ: Basic
           Features and Issues of a Biblical Theology of the New Testament,"
           HBT 1 (1980): 161-90.

0689   Jerome D. Quinn, "Tertullian and 1 Timothy 5:22 on Imposing
           Hands," *StudPat* 21 (1987): 268-70.

redaction criticism
0690   Percy N. Harrison, "The Pastoral Epistles and Duncan's Ephesian
           Theory," *NTS* 2 (1956): 250-61.

0691   André Lemaire, "Pastoral Epistles: Redaction and Theology," *BTB* 2
           (1972): 25-42.

0692   Peter Trummer, "Mantel und Schriften, 2 Tim 4:13: zur Interpretation
           einer persönlichen Notiz in den Pastoralbriefen," *BZ* N.S. 18 (1974):
           193-207.

0693   Jerome Murphy-O'Connor, "Redactional Angels in 1 Timothy 3:16,"
           RB 91 (1984): 178-87.

0694   Christian Grappe, "Essai sur l'arrière-plan Pascal des récits de la
           dernière nuit de Jésus," *RHPR* 65 (1985): 105-25.

regeneration
0695   Michael A. G. Haykin, "The Fading Vision: The Spirit and Freedom
           in the Pastoral Epistles," *EQ* 57 (1985): 291-305.

0696   John S. Pobee, "Human Transformation: A Biblical View," *MS* 2
           (1985): 5-9.

relation to Old Testament
0697   Charles M. Nielsen, "Scripture in the Pastoral Epistles," *PRS* 7
           (1980): 4-23.

0698 Peter Stuhlmacher, "The Gospel of Reconciliation in Christ: Basic Features and Issues of a Biblical Theology of the New Testament," *HBT* 1 (1980): 161-90.

0699 A. T. Hanson, "The Use of Scripture in the Pastoral Epistles and the Catholic Epistles," *The Living Utterances of God: The New Testament Exegesis of the Old*. London: Darton, Longman and Todd, 1983. Pp. 133-58.

0700 Mark A. Seifrid, "Paul's Approach to the Old Testament in Romans 10:6-8," *TriJ* N.S. 6 (1985): 3-37.

0701 Jouette Bassler, "Adam, Eve, and the Pastor: The Use of Genesis 2-3 in the Pastoral Epistles," in Gregory A. Robbins, ed., *Genesis 1-3 in the History of Exegesis: Intrigue in the Garden*. Lewiston NY: Edwin Mellen Press, 1988. Pp. 43-65.

0702 B. Paul Wolfe, "Scripture in the Pastoral Epistles: Pre-Marcion Marcionism?" *PRS* 16 (1989): 5-16.

0703 Klaus Berger, "Neutestamentliche Texte im Lichte der Weisheitsschrift aus der Geniza von Alt-Kairo," in Wolfgang Haase, ed., *Principat* 26,1: *Religion (vorkonstantinisches Christentum: Neues Testament*. New York: de Gruyter, 1992. Pp. 412-28.

0704 B. Paul Wolfe, *The Place and Use of Scripture in the Pastoral Epistles*. Ann Arbor MI: University Microfilms, 1993.

0705 R. G. Gruenler, "The Mission-Lifestyle Setting of 1 Timothy 2:8-15," *JETS* 41 (1998): 215-38.

resurrection

0706 William L. Lane, "1 Timothy 4:1-3: An Early Instance of Over-Realized Eschatology?" *NTS* 11 (1965): 164-67.

0707 Rudolf Schnackenburg, "Christologie des Neuen Testamentes," in Johannes Feiner and Magnus Löhrer, eds., *Mysterium salutis, 3/1: das Christusereignis*. Einsiedeln: Benziger Verlag, 1970. Pp. 230-388.

rhetoric

0708 Tom Thatcher, "The Relational Matrix of the Pastoral Epistles," *JETS* 38 (1995): 41-45.

0709 M. Harding, *Tradition and Rhetoric in the Pastoral Epistles*. Frankfurt: Lang, 1998.

righteousness
0710 Curtis C. Mitchell, "Why Keep Bothering God: The Case for Persisting in Prayer," *CT* 29 (1985): 33-34.

sex
0711 Randolph A. Nelson, "Homosexuality and Social Ethics," *WW* 5 (1985): 380-94.

0712 Richard B. Hays, "Relations Natural and Unnatural: A Response to J. Boswell's Exegesis of Romans 1," *JRE* 14 (1986): 184-215.

sin
0713 Jack Levison, "Is Eve to Blame: A Contextual Analysis of Sirach 25:24," *CBQ* 47 (1985): 617-23.

siociology
0714 D. C. Verner, *The Household of God: The Social World of the Pastoral Epistles*. SBL Dissertation Series #71. Chico CA: Scholars Press, 1983.

slavery
0715 Alfons Weiser, "Titus 2 als Gemeindeparänese," in Helmut Merklein, ed., *Neues Testament und Ethik* (festschrift for Rudolf Schnackenburg). Freiburg: Herder, 1989. Pp. 397-414.

sociology
0716 Reggie M. Kidd, *Wealth and Beneficence in the Pastoral Epistles: A "Bourgeois" form of Early Christianity?* Atlanta: Scholars Press, 1990.

0717 John S. McDermott, *The Quest for Community Stabilization: A Social Science Interpretation of the Pastoral Epistles*. Ann Arbor MI: U.M.I., 1991.

0718 Otto E. Bangerter, "Les veuves des epîtres pastorales: modèle d'un ministère féminin dans l'eglise ancienne," *FV* 83 (1984): 27-45.

0719 Jürgen Denker, "Identidad y mundo vivencial (Lebenswelt): en torno a Marcos 10:35-45 y Timoteo 2:5s," *RevB* 46 (1984): 159-69.

0720   Ferdinand Hahn, "Grundfragen von Charisma und Amt in der gegenwärtigen neutestamentlichen Forschung: Fragestellungen aus evangelischer Sicht," in Trutz Rendtorff, ed., *Charisma und Institution*. Gütersloh: Verlaghaus Gerd Mohn, 1985. Pp. 335-49.

0721   Thomas S. Caulley, "Fighting the Good Fight: The Pastoral Epistles in Canonical-Critical Perspective," *SBLSP* 26 (1987): 550-64.

0722   Walter F. Taylor, "1 Timothy 3:1-7: The Public Side of Ministry," *TSR* 14 (1992): 5-17.

0723   David Horrell, "Converging Ideologies: Berger and Luckmann and the Pastoral Epistles," *JSNT* 50 (1993): 85-103.

0724   Thomas R. Schreiner, "An Interpretation of 1 Timothy 2:9-15: A Dialogue with Scholarship," in Andreas J. Köstenberger, et al., eds., *Women in the Church: A Fresh Analysis of 1 Timothy 2:9-15*. Grand Rapids: Baker Book House, 1995. Pp. 105-54.

Son of Man
0725   Jürgen Denker, "Identidad y mundo vivencial (Lebenswelt): en torno a Marcos 10:35-45 y Timoteo 2:5s," *RevB* 46 (1984): 159-69.

soteriology
0726   Ivan Pancovski, "Tugend: Weg zum Heil," *OS* 32 (1983): 105-16.

0727   Jarl Ulrichsen, "Noen bemerkninger til 1 Tim 2:15," *NTT* 84 (1983): 19-25.

0728   Robert Javelet, "Marie, la femme médiatrice," *RevSR* 58 (1984): 162-71.

0729   C. Samuel Storms, "Defining the Elect: A Review Article," *JETS* 27 (1984): 205-18.

0730   P. Trokhin, "Hope and Salvation in the Holy Scripture of the New Testament," *JMosP* 8 (1984): 67-73.

0731   Michael R. Austin, "Salvation and the Divinity of Jesus," *ET* 96 (1985): 271-75.

0732   Gail Peterson Corrington, "Salvation, Celibacy, and Power: 'Divine Women' in Late Antiquity," *SBLSP* 24 (1985): 321-25.

0733 Luis F. Ladaria, "Dispensatio en S Hilario de Poitiers," *Greg* 66 (1985): 429-55.

0734 Malcolm J. McVeigh, "The Fate of Those Who've Never Heard: It Depends," *EMQ* 21 (1985): 370-79.

0735 John S. Pobee, "Human Transformation: A Biblical View," *MS* 2 (1985): 5-9.

0736 P. H. Towner, "The Present Age in the Eschatology of the Pastoral Epistles," *NTS* 32 (1986): 427-48.

0737 Geoffrey Wainwright, "Praying for Kings: The Place of Human Rulers in the Divine Plan of Salvation," *ExA* 2 (1986): 117-27.

0738 Krijn A. van der Jagt, "Women are Saved through Bearing Children," *BT* 39 (1988): 201-208.

0739 Steven M. Baugh, "Savior of All People: 1 Timothy 4:10 in Context," *WTJ* 54 (1992): 331-40.

0740 David R. Kimberley, "1 Timothy 2:15: A Possible Understanding of a Difficult Text," *JETS* 35 (1992): 481-86.

0741 Jarl Ulrichsen, "Heil durch Kindergebären: zu 1 Tim 2:15 und seiner syrischen Version," in René Kieffer, ed., *SEÅ* 58 (1993): Pp. 99-104.

0742 Lowell C. Green, "Universal Salvation according to the Lutheran Reformers," *LQ* 9 (1995): 281-300.

spirit

0743 Jerome D. Quinn, "On the Terminology for Faith, Truth, Teaching, and the Spirit in the Pastoral Epistles: A Summary," in Paul C. Empie, et al., eds., *Teaching Authority and Infallibility in the Church: Lutherans and Catholics in Dialogue VI*. Minneapolis: Augsburg Publishing House, 1978. Pp. 232-37.

spiritual gifts

0744 Jerome D. Quinn, "The Holy Spirit in the Pastoral Epistles," in Daniel Durken, ed., *Sin, Salvation and the Spirit*. Collegeville MN: Liturgical Press, 1979. Pp. 345-68.

0745   Ronald Y. K. Fung, "Charismatic Versus Organized Ministry: An Examination of an Alleged Antithesis," *EQ* 52 (1980): 195-214.

0746   Gerald G. Small, "The Use of Spiritual Gifts in the Ministry of Oversight," *CEJ* 1 (1980): 21-34.

0747   Ivan Havener, "Charisms and Ordered Ministries in the New Testament," in Daniel C. Brockopp, et al., eds., *Church and Ministry: Chosen Race, Royal Priesthood, Holy Nation, God's Own People.* Valparaiso IN: Institute of Liturgical Studies, 1982. Pp. 29-46.

0748   Ronald Y. K. Fung, "Function or Office: A Survey of the New Testament Evidence," *ERT* 8 (1984): 16-39.

0749   Kenneth B. Steinhauser, "Authority in the Primitive Church," *PatByzR* 3 (1984): 89-100.

0750   John J. Kilgallen, "Reflections on *charisma(ta)* in the New Testament," *SM* 41 (1992): 289-323.

textual criticism

0751   C. Maurer, "Eine Textvariante klärt die Entstehungegschichte der Pastoralbriefe auf," *TZ* 3 (1947): 321-37.

0752   R. J. A. Sheriffs, "Note on a Verse in the New English Bible," *EQ* 34 (1962): 91-95.

0753   A. T. Hanson, "The Domestication of Paul: A Study in the Development of Early Christian Theology," *BJRL* 63 (1981): 402-18.

0754   Jarl Ulrichsen, "Heil durch Kindergebären: zu 1 Tim 2:15 und seiner syrischen Version," in René Kieffer, ed., *SEÅ* 58 (1993): Pp. 99-104.

0755   J. K. Elliott, "A Greek-Coptic (Sahidic) Fragment of Titus-Philemon (0205)," *NovT* 36 (1994): 183-95.

0756   J. Duff, "P46 and the Pastorals: A Misleading Consensus," *NTS* 44 (1998): 578-90.

truth

0757   Georg Kretschmar, "Der paulinische Glaube in den Pastoralbriefen," in Ferdinand Hahn and Hans Klein, eds., *Glaube im Neuen Testament* (festschrift for Ehren von Hermann Binder). Neukirchen-Vluyn: Neukirchener Verlag, 1982. Pp. 115-40.

0758 Jesse Sell, "The Knowledge of the Truth," in Tito Orlandi and Frederik Wisse, eds., *Acts of the Second International Congress of Coptic Studies*. Rome: CIM, 1985. Pp. 345-53.

wealth

0759 Reggie M. Kidd, *Wealth and Beneficence in the Pastoral Epistles: A "Bourgeois" form of Early Christianity?* Atlanta: Scholars Press, 1990.

0760 Ken Smith, "The Stewardship of Money," *FundJ* 4 (1985): 31-33.

0761 Werner Bieder, "Reiche als Mitarbeiter der Befreiung?" *ZMiss* 17 (1991): 66-69.

0762 Peter Dschulnigg, "Warnung vor Reichtum und Ermahnung der Reichen: 1 Tim 6:6-10,17-19 im Rahmen des Schlussteils 6:3-21," *BZ* N.S. 37 (1993): 60-77.

wisdom

0763 Otto Knoch, "Torheit, Weisheit und Besonnenheit als Grundhaltungen des Christen: eine vergleichende Studie über die Entfaltung einer paulinischen Glaubensaussage in den Schriften der Paulusschule," in Walter Baier, et al., eds., *Weisheit Gottes - Weisheit der Welt* (festschrift for Joseph Kardinal Ratzinger). 2 volumes. Sankt Ottilien: EOS Verlag, 1987. Pp. 441-51.

women

0764 E. Kähler, "Die Stellung der Frau in den Pastoralbriefen," in *Die Frau in den paulinischen Briefen*. Zurich: Gotthelf, 1960. Pp. 141-71.

0765 S. Jebb, "Suggested Interpretation of 1 Titus 2:15," *ET* 81 (1970): 221-22.

0766 Aida B. Spencer, "Eve at Ephesus," *JETS* 17 (1974): 215-22.

0767 S. Philsy, "*Diakonia* of Women in the New Testament," *IJT* 32 (1983): 110-18.

0768 Eva C. Topping, "Patriarchal Prejudice and Pride in Greek Christianity: Some Notes on Origins," *JMGS* 1 (1983): 7-17.

0769   Jarl Ulrichsen, "Noen bemerkninger til 1 Tim 2:15," *NTT* 84 (1983): 19-25.

0770   Otto E. Bangerter, "Les veuves des epîtres pastorales: modèle d'un ministère féminin dans l'eglise ancienne," *FV* 83 (1984): 27-45.

0771   George W. Knight, "αὐθεντέω in Reference to Women in 1 Timothy 2:12," *NTS* 30 (1984): 143-57.

0772   Gail Peterson Corrington, "Salvation, Celibacy, and Power: 'Divine Women' in Late Antiquity," *SBLSP* 24 (1985): 321-25.

0773   Pui Lan Kwok, "The Feminist Hermeneutics of Elisabeth Schüssler Fiorenza: An Asian Feminist Response," *EAJT* 3 (1985): 147-53.

0774   Jack Levison, "Is Eve to Blame: A Contextual Analysis of Sirach 25:24," *CBQ* 47 (1985): 617-23.

0775   Rosemary Radford Ruether, "The Liberation of Christology from Patriarchy," *RIL* 2 (1985): 116-28.

0776   Frank Stagg, "The Gospel, Haustafel, and Women: Mark 1:1; Colossians 3:18-4:1," *FM* 2 (1985): 59-63.

0777   Lyle Vander Broek, "Women and the Church: Approaching Difficult Passages," *RR* 38 (1985): 225-31.

0778   Alan Padgett, "The Pauline Rationale for Submission: Biblical Feminism and the *Hina* Clauses of Titus 2:1-10," *EQ* 59 (1987): 39-52.

0779   Alan Padgett, "Wealthy Women at Ephesus: 1 Timothy 2:8-15 in Social Context," *Int* 41 (1987): 19-31.

0780   Robert W. Allison, "Let Women Be Silent in the Churches (1 Corinthians 14:33b-36): What Did Paul Really Say, and What Did It Mean?" *JSNT* 32 (1988): 27-60.

0781   Jouette Bassler, "Adam, Eve, and the Pastor: The Use of Genesis 2-3 in the Pastoral Epistles," in Gregory A. Robbins, ed., *Genesis 1-3 in the History of Exegesis: Intrigue in the Garden*. Lewiston NY: Edwin Mellen Press, 1988. Pp. 43-65.

0782 Krijn A. van der Jagt, "Women Are Saved through Bearing Children," *BT* 39 (1988): 201-208.

0783 Dorothy Kelley Patterson, "Why I Believe Southern Baptist Churches Should not Ordain Women," *BHH* 23 (1988): 56-62.

0784 Bruce W. Winter, "Providentia for the Widows of 1 Timothy 5:3-16," *TynB* 39 (1988): 83-99.

0785 Paul W. Barnett, "Wives and Women's Ministry (1 Timothy 2:11-15)," *EQ* 61 (1989): 225-38.

0786 Tarsicius J. van Bavel, "Women as the Image of God in Augustine's De trinitate XII," in Adolar Zumkeller, ed., *Signum pietatis* (festschrift for Cornelius Petrus Mayer). Würzburg: Augustinus-Verlag, 1989. Pp. 267-88.

0787 Carol J. Westphal, "Coming Home," *RR* 42 (1989): 177-88.

0788 Paul W. Barnett, "Women in the Church," in Nichols, Alan, ed., *The Bible and Women's Ministry: An Australian Dialogue*. Canberra, Australia: Acorn Press, 1990. Pp. 49-64.

0789 Bruce Barron, "Putting Women in Their Place: 1 Timothy 2 and Evangelical Views of Women in Church Leadership," *JETS* 33 (1990): 451-59.

0790 Gordon D. Fee, "Issues in Evangelical Hermeneutics III: The Great Watershed—Intentionality and Particularity/Eternality: 1 Timothy 2:8-15 as a Test Case," *Crux* 26 (1990): 31-37.

0791 Kevin Giles, "Response," in Alan Nichols, ed., *The Bible and Women's Ministry: An Australian Dialogue*. Canberra, Australia: Acorn Press, 1990. Pp. 65-87.

0792 Timothy J. Harris, "Why Did Paul Mention Eve's Deception? A Critique of P. W. Barnett's Interpretation of 1 Timothy 2," *EQ* 62 (1990): 335-52.

0793 Peter Jensen, "Using Scripture," in Nichols, Alan, ed., *The Bible and Women's Ministry: An Australian Dialogue*. Canberra, Australia: Acorn Press, 1990. Pp. 1-16.

0794   Gloria Neufeld Redekop, "Let the Women Learn: 1 Timothy 2:8-15 Reconsidered," *SR* 19 (1990): 235-45.

0795   Sharon H. Gritz, "The Role of Women in the Church," in Paul A. Basden and David S. Dockery, eds., *The People of God: Essays on the Believers' Church.* Nashville: Broadman Press, 1991. Pp. 299-314.

0796   Arthur Rowe, "Hermeneutics and 'Hard Passages' in the NT on the Role of Women in the Church: Issues from Recent Literature," *EpRev* 18 (1991): 82-88.

0797   Ann L. Bowman, "Women in Ministry: An Exegetical Study of 1 Timothy 2:11-15," *BSac* 149 (1992): 193-213.

0798   Gordon P. Hugenberger, "Women in Church Office: Hermeneutics or Exegesis? A Survey of Approaches to 1 Timothy 2:8-15," *JETS* 35 (1992): 341-60.

0799   David R. Kimberley, "1 Timothy 2:15: A Possible Understanding of a Difficult Text," *JETS* 35 (1992): 481-86.

0800   Andrew C. Perriman, "What Eve Did, What Women Shouldn't Do: The Meaning of *authenteo* in 1 Timothy 2:12," *TynB* 44 (1993): 129-42.

0801   Ronald W. Pierce, "Evangelicals and Gender Roles in the 1990s: 1 Timothy 2:8-15: A Test Case," *JETS* 36 (1993): 343-55.

0802   Stanley E. Porter, "What Does it Mean to be 'Saved by Childbirth'?" *JSNT* 49 (1993): 87-102.

0803   Robert W. Schaibley, "Gender Considerations on the Pastoral Office: In Light of 1 Corinthians 14:33-36 and 1 Timothy 2:8-14," *Logia* 2 (1993): 48-54; 3 (1994): 45-51.

0804   Steven M. Baugh, "The Apostle among the Amazons," *WTJ* 56 (1994): 153-71.

0805   Stephen Moyer, "Expounding 1 Timothy 2:8-15," *VoxE* 24 (1994): 91-102.

0806   Robert L. Saucy, "Women's Prohibition to Teach Men: An Investigation into Its Meaning and Contemporary Application," *JETS* 37 (1994): 79-97.

0807   Ben Wiebe, "Two Texts on Women: A Test of Interpretation," *HBT* 16 (1994): 54-85.

0808   Harold O. J. Brown, "The New Testament against Itself: 1 Timothy 2:9-15 and the 'Breakthrough' of Galatians 3:28," in Andreas J. Köstenberger, et al., eds., *Women in the Church: A Fresh Analysis of 1 Timothy 2:9-15*. Grand Rapids: Baker Book House, 1995. Pp. 197-208.

0809   Thomas R. Schreiner, "An Interpretation of 1 Timothy 2:9-15: A Dialogue with Scholarship," in Andreas J. Köstenberger, et al., eds., *Women in the Church: A Fresh Analysis of 1 Timothy 2:9-15*. Grand Rapids: Baker Book House, 1995. Pp. 105-54.

0810   Jennifer H. Stoefel, "Women Deacons in 1 Timothy: A Linguistic and Literary Look at 'Women Likewise . . . '," *NTS* 41 (1995): 442-57.

0811   M. Lynn Gannett, "Older Women/Younger Women: The Implementation of Titus 2," in Kenneth O. Gangel and James C. Wilhoit, eds., *The Christian Educator's Handbook on Family Life Education*. Grand Rapids: Baker Book House, 1996. Pp. 83-95.

0812   Andreas J. Köstenberger, "The Crux of the Matter: Paul's Pastoral Pronouncements Regarding Women's Roles in 1 Timothy 2:9-15," *FM* 14 (1996): 24-48.

0813   P. H. Towner, "Feminist Approaches to the New Testament: With Timothy 2:8-15 as a Test Case," *JianD* 7 (1997): 91-111.

word studies
0814   S. Bedale, "The Meaning of *kephalê* in the Pauline Epistles," *JTS* 5 (1954): 211-15.

0815   Werner Foerster, "Eysebeia in den Pastoralbriefen," *NTS* 5 (1958-1959): 213-18.

0816   L. L. Lancaster, "The Theology of the Diaconate," *IJT* 8 (1959): 151-55.

0817 J. K. Elliott, *"Didomi* in 2 Timothy," *JTS* 19 (1968): 621-23.

0818 Peter Trummer, "Einehe nach den Pastoralbriefen: zum Verständnis der Termini μιᾶς γυναικὸς ἀνήρ und ἑνὸς ἀνδρος γυνή," *Bib* 51 (1970): 471-84.

0819 Otfried Hofius, "Zur Auslegungsgeschichte von presbyterion 1 Tim 4:14," *ZNW* 62 (1971): 128-29.

0820 John P. Meier, "Presbyteros in the Pastoral Epistles," *CBQ* 35 (1973): 323-45.

0821 John J. O'Rourke, "Some Considerations about Attempts at Statistical Analysis of the Pauline Corpus," *CBQ* 35 (1973): 483-90.

0822 Neil J. McEleney, "Vice Lists of the Pastoral Epistles," *CBQ* 36 (1974): 203-19.

0823 Otto Merk, "Glaube und Tat in den pastoralbriefen," *ZNW* 66 (1975): 91-102.

0824 Norbert Brox, *"Prophētia* im ersten Timotheusbrief," *BZ* 20 (1976): 229-32.

0825 Jerome D. Quinn, "On the Terminology for Faith, Truth, Teaching, and the Spirit in the Pastoral Epistles: A Summary," in Paul C. Empie, et al., eds., *Teaching Authority and Infallibility in the Church: Lutherans and Catholics in Dialogue VI.* Minneapolis: Augsburg Publishing House, 1978. Pp. 232-37.

0826 Eduard Lohse, "Episkopos in den Pastoralbriefen," in Otto Böcher, et al., *Kirche und Bibel: Festgabe für Bischof Eduard Schick.* Paderborn: Ferdinand Schönigh, 1979. Pp. 225-32.

0827 Lorenz Obenlinner, "Die "Epiphaneia" des Heilswillens Gottes in Christus Jesus: zur Grundstruktur der Christologie der Pastoralbriefe," *ZNW* 71 (1980): 192-213.

0828 Neal F. McBride and W. Creighton Marlowe, "Biblical Distinctives between the Content and Character of Teaching and Preaching," *CEJ* 1 (1981): 68-74.

0829 Stephen Westerholm, "The Law and the 'Just Man' (1 Timothy 1:3-11)," *StTheol* 36 (1982): 79-95.

0830 Ivan Pancovski, "Tugend: Weg zum Heil," *OS* 32 (1983): 105-16.

0831 Richard D. Patterson, "Pouring out," *FundJ* 2 (1983): 19.

0832 Carl Diemer, "Deacons and Other Endangered Species: A Look at the Biblical Office of Deacon," *FundJ* 3 (1984): 21-24.

0833 Kendell H. Easley, "The Pauline Usage of *pneumati* as a Reference to the Spirit of God," *JETS* 27 (1984): 299-313.

0834 Abraham J. Malherbe, "In Season and Out of Season: 2 Timothy 4:2 [eukairos akairos]," *JBL* 103 (1984): 235-43.

0835 Rolf Gögler, "Inkarnationsglaube und Bibeltheologie bei Origenes," *TQ* 165 (1985): 82-94.

0836 Luis F. Ladaria, "Dispensatio en S Hilario de Poitiers," *Greg* 66 (1985): 429-55.

0837 Richard D. Patterson, "In Remembrance of Me," *FundJ* 4 (1985): 31.

0838 Jacques Schlosser, "La didascalie et ses agents dans les épîtres pastorales," *RevSR* 59 (1985): 81-94.

0839 Mark A. Seifrid, "Paul's Approach to the Old Testament in Romans 10:6-8," *TriJ* N.S. 6 (1985): 3-37.

0840 P. H. Towner, "The Present Age in the Eschatology of the Pastoral Epistles," *NTS* 32 (1986): 427-48.

0841 Alan Padgett, "The Pauline Rationale for Submission: Biblical Feminism and the *Hina* Clauses of Titus 2:1-10," *EQ* 59 (1987): 39-52.

0842 David F. Wright, "Translating *arsenokoitai* (1 Corinthians 6:9; 1 Timothy 1:10)," *VC* 41 (1987): 396-98.

0843 Krijn A. van der Jagt, "Women Are Saved through Bearing Children," *BT* 39 (1988): 201-208.

0844   Antonio Piñero, "Sobre el sentido de θεόπνευστος: 2 Tim 3:16," *FilN* 1 (1988): 143-53.

0845   Leland E. Wilshire, "The *TLG* Computer and Further Reference to αὐθεντέω in 1 Timothy 2:12," *NTS* 34 (1988): 120-34.

0846   Karl P. Donfried, "Paul as Skenopoios and the use of the codex in early Christianity," in Karl Kertelge, eds., *Christus bezeugen* (festschrift for Wolfgang Trilling. Leipzig: St. Benno, 1989. Pp. 249-56.

0847   Georg Schöllgen, "Die diple time von 1 Timothy 5:17," *ZNW* 80 (1989): 232-39.

0848   Frederick E. Brenk, "Old Wineskins Recycled: *autarkeia* in 1 Timothy 6:5-10," *FilN* 3 (1990): 39-52.

0849   Everett Ferguson, "*Topos* in 1 Timothy 2:8," *RQ* 33 (1991): 64-73.

0850   James B. De Young, "The Source and New Testament Meaning of *arsenokoitai,* with Implications for Christian Ethics and Ministry," *MSJ* 3 (1992): 191-215.

0851   Andrew C. Perriman, "What Eve Did, What Women Shouldn't Do: The Meaning of *authenteo* in 1 Timothy 2:12," *TynB* 44 (1993): 129-42.

0852   John J. Wainwright, "*Eusebeia*: Syncretism or Conservative Contextualization?" *EQ* 65 (1993): 211-24.

0853   Leland E. Wilshire, "1 Timothy 2:12 Revisited," *EQ* 65 (1993): 43-55.

0854   R. Alastair Campbell, "Identifying the Faithful Sayings in the Pastoral Epistles," *JSNT* 54 (1994): 73-86.

0855   Robert L. Saucy, "Women's Prohibition to Teach Men: An Investigation into Its Meaning and Contemporary Application," *JETS* 37 (1994): 79-97.

0856   H. Scott Baldwin, "A Difficult Word: αὐθεντέω in 1 Timothy 2:12," in Andreas J. Köstenberger, et al., eds., *Women in the Church: A*

Fresh Analysis of 1 Timothy 2:9-15. Grand Rapids: Baker Book House, 1995. Pp. 65-80.

0857   R. Alastair Campbell, *"Kai malista oikeion*—A New Look at 1 Timothy 5:8," *NTS* 41 (1995): 157-60.

0858   Andreas J. Köstenberger, "A Complex Sentence Structure in 1 Timothy 2:12," in Andreas J. Köstenberger, et al., eds., *Women in the Church: A Fresh Analysis of 1 Timothy 2:9-15.* Grand Rapids: Baker Book House, 1995. Pp. 81-103.

0859   J. Lionel North, " 'Human Speech' in Paul and the Paulines: The Investigation and Meaning of *anthropinos o logos,*" *NovT* 37 (1995): 50-67.

0860   Dale B. Martin, *"Arsenokoitês* and *Malakos*: Meanings and Consequences," in Robert L. Brawley, ed., *Biblical Ethics and Homosexuality: Listening to Scripture.* Louisville: Westminster/John Knox Press, 1996. Pp. 117-36.

0861   E. Butzer, "Die Witwen der Pastoralbriefe," *TexteK* 20 (1998): 35-52.

0862   T. Söding, "Gottes Menschenfreundlichkeit: Eine exegetische Meditation von Titus 3," *GeistL* 71 (1998): 410-422.

0863   J. A. Harrill, "The Vice of Slave Dealers in Greco-Roman Society: The Use of a *Topos* in 1 Timothy 1:10," *JBL* 118 (1999): 97-122.

0864   B. R. Keller, "Timothy 5:17—Did All πρεσβύτεροι Proclaim God's Word?" *WLQ* 96 (1999): 43-49

PART THREE

Commentaries

0865   Alfred Plummer, *The Pastoral Epistles*. New York: A.C. Armstrong, 1900.

0866   George B. Stevens, *The Messages of the Apostles: The Apostolic Ddiscourses in the Book of Acts and the General and Pastoral Epistles of the New Testament Arranged in Chronological Order, Analyzed, and Freely Rendered in Paraphrase*. New York: Scribner, 1900.

0867   Robert F. Horton, *The Pastoral Epistles Timothy and Titus*. New York: Henry Frowde, 1901.

0868   J. P. Lilley, *The Pastoral Epistles: A New Translation with Introduction, Commentary, and Appendix*. Edinburgh: T. & T. Clark, 1901.

0869   Bernhard Weiss, *Die Briefe Pauli an Timotheus und Titus*. Göttingen: Vandenhoeck und Ruprecht, 1902.

0870   George W. Clark, *Galatians, Ephesians, Philippians, Colossians, I and II Thessalonians, I and II Timothy, Titus and Philemon: A Popular Commentary upon a Critical Basis, Especially Designed for Pastors and Sunday Schools*. Philadelphia: American Baptist Publication Society, 1903.

0871   Gustav Wohlenberg, *Die Pastoralbriefe: 9 (der erste Timotheus-, der Titus- und der zweite Timotheusbrief)*. Leipzig: A. Deichert, 1906.

0872   J. E. Belser, *Die Briefe des Apostels Paulus an Timotheus und Titus*. Freiburg im Breisgau: Herder, 1907.

0873   Edward T. Horn, *Annotations on the Epistle of Paul to the Ephesians, Philippians, Colossians Thessalonians*. New York: Charles Scribners Sons, 1911.

0874   Gustav Wohlenberg, *Die Pastoralbriefe der erste Timotheus-, der Titus-, und der zweite Timotheusbrief*. 2. verbesserte und vermehrte Aufl. Leipzig, Deichert, 1911.

0875   N. J. D. White, *The First and Second Epistles to Timothy and the Epistle to Titus*. Volume 4. The Expositor's Greek Testament. London: Hodder and Stoughton, 1912.

0876   Ernest F. Brown, *The Pastoral Epistles*. London: Methuen, 1917.

0877   H. M. van Nes, *Paulus' brieven aan de Galatiers, Efeziers, Filippenzen, Kolossenzen, Thessalonicenzen (1 en 2), Timotheus (1 en 2), Titus en Filemon*. Groningen: Walters, 1919.

0878   R. St. John Parry, *The Pastoral Epistles with Introduction Text and Commentary*. Cambridge: University Press, 1920.

0879   Charles R. Erdman, *The Pastoral Epistles of Paul: An Exposition*. Philadelphia: Westminster Press, 1923.

0880   Walter Lock, *A Critical and Exegetical Commentary on the Pastoral Epistles*. Edinburgh: T. & T. Clark, 1924.

0881   A. E. Humphreys, *The Epistles to Timothy and Titus*. Cambridge UK: The University Press, 1925.

0882   Ernest F. Scott, *The Pastoral Epistles*. New York: Harper, 1936.

0883   Robert Falconer, *The Pastoral Epistles: Introduction, Translation and Notes*. Oxford: Clarendon Press, 1937.

0884   Alexander Maclaren, *Second Timothy, Titus, Philemon and Hebrews: Hebrews, Epistle of James*. Grand Rapids MI: Eerdmans, 1944.

0885   R. C. H. Lenski, *The Interpretation of St. Paul's Epistles to the Colossians, to the Thessalonians, to the Timothy, to Titus and to Philemon*. Columbus OH: Wartburg Press, 1946.

0886   Burton S. Easton, *The Pastoral Epistles: Introduction, Translation, Commentary and Word Studies*. New York: Scribner's, 1947.

0887   E. L. Smelik, *Der wegen der kerk: de brieven aan Timotheus, Titus en Filemon*. 2nd ed. Nijkerk: G. F. Callenbach, 1947.

0888   C. Spicq, *Saint Paul: les Épîtres pastorales*. Paris: J. Gabalda, 1947.

0889   A. Boudou, *Les épîtres pastorales*. Paris: Beauchesne, 1950.

0890   Cornelis Bouma, *De brieven van den apostel Paulus aan Timotheus en Titus*. 2nd ed. Kampen: Kok, 1953.

0891   P. De Ambroggi, *Le Epistole Pastorali di S. Paolo a Timoteo e a Tito*. Torino: Marietti, 1953.

0892   William Hendriksen, *New Testament Commentary: 1-2 Timothy. Titus*. Volume 4. Grand Rapids: Baker Book House, 1953.

0893 Kenneth S. Wuest, *The Pastoral Epistles in the Greek New Testament for the English Reader*. Grand Rapids: Eerdmans, 1953.

0894 Hermann Riess, *Der Philemon-, Titus- und 2. Timotheusbrief*. Stuttgart: Kreuz-Verlag, 1956.

0895 Donald Guthrie, *The Pastoral Epistles: An Introduction and Commentary*. Grand Rapids: Eerdmans, 1957.

0896 Walter Warth, *Die beiden Timotheusbriefe, der Titus brief, der Philemonbrief*. Stuttgart: Quell, 1957.

0897 Adolf von Schlatter, *Die Kirche der Griechen im Urteil des Paulus: eine Auslegung seiner Briefe an Timotheus und Titus*. 2. Aufl. Stuttgart: Calwer Verlag, 1958.

0898 Wilhelm Knappe, *Der Briefe an Timotheus und Titus*. Kassel: J.G. Oncken, 1959.

0899 Hebert Roux, *Les Épîtres pastorales; commentaire de I et II Timothee et Tite*. Paris: Editions Labor et Fides, 1959.

0900 William Barclay, *The Letters to Timothy, Titus, and Philemon*. Edinburgh: Saint Andrew Press, 1960.

0901 A. R. C. Leaney, *The Epistles to Timothy, Titus, and Philemon: Introduction and Commentary*. London: SCM Press, 1960.

0902 Paul F. Barackman, *The Epistles to Timothy and Titus*. Proclaiming the New Testament #6. Grand Rapids: Baker, 1962.

0903 Maxwell R. Robinson, *A Commentary on the Pastoral Epistles*. Madras: Christian Literature Society, 1962.

0904 Joachim Jeremias, *Die Briefe an Timotheus und Titus. Der Brief an die Hebräer*. Göttingen, Vandenhoeck & Ruprecht, 1963.

0905 J. N. D. Kelly, *A Commentary on the Pastoral Epistles; I Timothy, II Timothy, Titus*. New York: Harper & Row, 1963.

0906 Holmes Rolston, *The First and Second Ltters of Paul to the Thessalonians; the First and Second letters of Paul to Timothy: the Letter of Paul to Titus; the Letter of Paul to Philemon*. Richmond VA: John Knox Press, 1963.

0907   Arthur P. Carleton, *Pastoral Epistles: A Commentary.* New York: Association Press, 1964.

0908   Gootfried Holtz, *Die Pastoralbriefe.* Berlin: Evangelische Verlagsanstalt, 1965.

0909   W. E. Vine, *The Epistles to Timothy and Titus: Faith and Conduct.* Grand Rapids: Zondervan, 1965.

0910   A. T. Hanson, *The Pastoral Letters: Commentary on the First and Second Letters to Timothy and the Letter to Titus.* Cambridge: University Press, 1966.

0911   Joseph Reuss, *Der Brief an Titus.* Dusseldorf, Patmos-Verlag, 1966.

0912   Herman N. Ridderbos, *De pastorale brieven.* Kampen: J. H. Kok, 1967.

0913   Franz J. Schierse, *Die Pastoralbriefe.* Düsseldorf: Patmos-Verlag, 1968.

0914   Pierre Dornier, *Les Épîtres pastorales.* Paris: J. Gabalda et Cie, 1969.

0915   Howard A. Moellering, *Concordia Commentary: 1 Timothy, 2 Timothy, Titus.* Saint Louis: Concordia Publishing House, 1970.

0916   Carl Spain, *The Letters of Paul to Timothy and Titus.* Austin TX: R. B. Sweet Co., 1970.

0917   Martin Dibelius and Hans Conzelmann, *The Pastoral Epistles: A Commentary on the Pastoral Epistles,* ed. Helmut Koester. Trans. Philip Buttolph and Adela Yarbro. Philadelphia: Fortress Press, 1972.

0918   A. Cousineau, *Les Pastorales: Traduction et commentaire.* Montréal: Éditions Paulines. 1974.

0919   Ronald A. Ward, *Commentary on 1 & 2 Timothy & Titus.* Waco TX: Word Books, 1974.

0920   Hans F. Burki, *Der zweite Brief des Paulus an Timotheus, die Briefe an Titus und an Philemon.* Wuppertal: Brockhaus, 1975.

0921   J. L. Houlden, *The Pastoral Epistles: I and II Timothy, Titus.* The Pelican New Testament Commentaries. Harmondsworth: Penguin, 1976.

0922 Victor Hasler, *Die Briefe an Timotheus und Titus.* Zurich: Theologischer Verlag, 1978.

0923 J. Paul Sampley, et al., *Ephesians, Colossians, 2 Thessalonians, the Pastoral Epistles.* Proclamation Commentaries. Philadelphia: Fortress Press, 1978.

0924 Robert J. Karris, *The Pastoral Epistles.* Wilmington: M. Glazier, 1979.

0925 Robert G. Bratcher, *A Translator's Guide to Paul's Letters to Timothy and to Titus.* New York: United Bible Societies, 1983.

0926 Jerome H. Neyrey, *First Timothy, Second Timothy, Titus, James, First Peter, Second Peter, Jude.* Collegeville MN: Liturgical Press, 1983.

0927 Gary W. Demarest, *The Communicator's Commentary. 1, 2 Thessalonians, 1, 2 Timothy, Titus.* Waco TX: Word Books, 1984.

0928 W. S. Duvekot, *De Pastorale Brieven. 1 en 2 Timotheüs en Titus.* Kampen: Kok, 1984.

0929 Arland J. Hultgren, *1-2 Timothy, Titus.* Minneapolis: Augsburg Publishing House, 1984.

0930 Maxie D. Dunnam, *1, 2 Thessalonians, 1, 2 Timothy, Titus.* The Communicator's Commentary Series #9. Waco TX: Word Books, 1985.

0931 Udo Borse, *1. und 2. Timotheusbrief: Titusbrief.* 2. Aufl. Stuttgart: Katholisches Bibelwerk, 1986.

0932 Rinaldo Fabris, *Le lettere pastorali.* Brescia: Editrice Queriniana, 1986.

0933 Gordon D. Fee, *1 and 2 Timothy, Titus.* New International Biblical Commentary #13. Peabody MS: Hendrickson Publishers, 1988.

0934 Otto Knoch, *1. und 2. Timotheusbrief.* Würzburg: Echter Verlag, 1988.

0935 C. den Boer, *De tweede brief van Paulus aan Timotheus: De brief van Paulus aan titus.* Kampen: Kok, 1989.

0936 Norbert Brox, *Die Pastoralbriefe: 1 Timotheus, 2 Timotheus, Titus.* 5. durchgesehene und erw. Aufl. Regensburg: Verlag F. Pustet, 1989.

0937   Thomas C. Oden, *First and Second Timothy and Titus*. Louisville: J. Knox Press, 1989.

0938   Carol K. Stockhausen, *Letters in the Pauline Tradition: Ephesians, Colossians, 1 Timothy, 2 Timothy, and Titus*. Wilmington DL: Glazier, 1989.

0939   Fritz Grunzweig, *Zweiter Timotheus-Brief, Titus- und Philemon-Brief.* Neuhausen-Stuttgart: Hannsler, 1990.

0940   Jerome D. Quinn, *The Letter to Titus: A New Translation with Notes and Commentary and an Introduction to Titus, I and II Timothy, the Pastoral Epistles*. New York: Doubleday, 1990.

0941   George W. Knight, *The Pastoral Epistles: A Commentary on the Greek Text*. Grand Rapids: Eerdmans, 1992.

0942   Thomas D. Lea, *1, 2 Timothy, Titus*. Nashville TN: Broadman Press, 1992.

0943   Bruce B. Barton, *1 Timothy, 2 Timothy, Titus*. Wheaton IL: Tyndale House Publishers, 1993.

0944   J. Paul Sampley, *The Deutero-Pauline Letters: Ephesians, Colossians, 2 Thessalonians, Timothy, Titus*. Minneapolis: Fortress Press, 1993.

0945   Georges Gander, *Les Epîtres dites "pastorales" de l'apôtre Paul: 1 Timothée, 2 Timothée, Tite, Philémon*. Saint-Légier: Editions Contrastes, 1994.

0946   C. Michael Moss, *1, 2 Timothy & Titus*. Joplin MO: College Press, 1994.

0947   Philip Towner, *1-2 Timothy & Titus*. Downers Grove IL: InterVarsity Press, 1994.

0948   Daniel C. Arichea and Howard A. Hatton, *A Handbook on Paul's Letters to Timothy and to Titus*. New York: United Bible Societies, 1995.

0949   Jouette Bassler, *1 Timothy, 2 Timothy, Titus*. Nashville TN: Abingdon Press, 1996.

0950   Margaret Davies, *The Pastoral Epistles*. Sheffield: Sheffield Academic, 1996.

0951   Lewis R. Donelson, *Colossians, Ephesians, First and Second Timothy, and Titus*. Louisville KY: Westminster John Knox Press, 1996.

0952   Michael Griffiths, *Timothy and Titus*. Grand Rapids MI: Baker Books, 1996.

0953   Luke T. Johnson, *Letters to Paul's Delegates: 1 Timothy, 2 Timothy, Titus*. Valley Forge PA: Trinity Press International, 1996.

0954   John MacArthur, *Titus*. Chicago: Moody Press, 1996.

0955   Lorenz Oberlinner, *Der Pastoralbriefe, dritte Folge: Kommentar zum Titusbrief*. Freiburg: Herder, 1996.

0956   John R. W. Stott, *Guard the Truth: The Message of 1 Timothy and Titus*. Downers Grove IL: InterVarsity Press, 1996.

Index

Ford, J. Massyngberde   0527
Frede, H. J.   0617
Fuller, J. W.   0218
Fung, Ronald Y. K.   0745, 0748
Gaide, G.   0030
Gander, Georges   0945
Gannett, M. Lynn   0811
Gartner, B.   0130
Gero, Stephen   0322
Giles, Kevin   0087, 0791
Glasscock, Ed   0116, 0376, 0472
Glorieux, Palémon   0040, 0439
Gögler, Rolf   0043, 0466, 0555, 0835
Goldstein, H.   0461
Goodwin, Mark J.   0175
Goulder, Michael D.   0653
Grappe, Christian   0243, 0440, 0679, 0694
Grayston, K.   0574
Grech, Prosper   0630
Green, Lowell C.   0044, 0742
Griffiths, Michael   0952
Griffths, Michael C.   0005, 0365
Gritz, Sharon H.   0072, 0795
Grounds, Vernon C.   0027
Gruenler, R. G.   0067, 0705
Grunzweig, Fritz   0939
Gundry, R. H.   0140
Guthrie, Donald   0895
Gutierrez, P.   0584
Hahn, Ferdinand   0467, 0720
Hall, D. R.   0274
Hann, Robert R.   0039, 0476
Hannah, Jack   0548
Hanson, A. T.   0045, 0099, 0131, 0307, 0327, 0424, 0618, 0663, 0699, 0753, 0910
Harding, M.   0709
Harrill, J. A.   0017, 0863
Harris, Timothy J.   0792
Harrison, Percy N.   0560, 0570, 0572, 0573, 0690

Harvey, A. E.   0216
Hasler, Victor   0435, 0922
Hatton, Howard A.   0948
Haufe, Günter   0489
Haulotte, Edgar   0152, 0509, 0553
Havener, Ivan   0747
Haykin, Michael A. G.   0024, 0163, 0178, 0262, 0282, 0410, 0536, 0695
Hays, Richard B.   0012, 0494, 0542, 0712
Hegermann, Harald   0589
Hellwig, Monika K.   0326
Hendriksen, William   0892
Hennecke, Edgar   0612
Herdan, G.   0574
Heth, William A.   0206
Hofius, Otfried   0181, 0819
Hofrichter, Peter   0633
Holman, Charles L   0415, 0538
Holtz, Gootfried   0908
Holzmeister, U.   0120, 0298, 0393
Horn, Edward T.   0873
Horrell, David   0723
Horton, Robert F.   0867
Houlden, J. L.   0921
Hugenberger, Gordon P.   0063, 0670, 0798
Hultgren, Arland J.   0929
Humphreys, A. E.   0881
Jaubert, A.   0129
Javelet, Robert   0046, 0518, 0728
Javierre, A. M.   0288
Jebb, S.   0104, 0765
Jensen, Peter   0227, 0793
Jeremias, Joachim   0904
Johnson, Luke T.   0523, 0953
Johnston, J.   0567
Junack, K.   0603
Kaestli, Jean D.   0650
Kähler, E.   0764
Karris, Robert J.   0591, 0924
Käsemann, Ernst   0240, 0251, 0477

Stuhlmacher, Peter   0486, 0688, 0698
Synge, Francis C.   0190
Synnes, Martin   0613
Taylor, Walter F.   0117, 0722
Tetz, Martin   0340
Thatcher, Tom   0708
Thiselton, Anthony C.   0381
Thomas, W. D.   0284
Thompson, Alvin   0289
Thompson, George H. P.   0296
Thurén, Jukka   0230, 0487
Thurston, Bonnie Bowman   0194
Topping, Eva C.   0086, 0552, 0768
Towner, P. H.   0066, 0484, 0485, 0516, 0652, 0736, 0813, 0840, 0947
Trokhin, P.   0038, 0547, 0730
Troxel, A. Burge   0221, 0464, 0471
Trummer, Peter   0121, 0127, 0201, 0366, 0379, 0611, 0620, 0666, 0692, 0818
Turnbull, Ralph G.   0581
Twomey, J. J.   0360
Ulrichsen, Jarl   0037, 0106, 0111, 0727, 0741, 0754, 0769
van Bavel, Tarsicius J.   0108, 0786
van Bruggen, J.   0621
van der Jagt, Krijn A.   0078, 0738, 0782, 0843
van Nes, H. M.   0877
Van Rensburg, Fika J. Janse   0151
Vander Broek, Lyle   0056, 0777
Vargha, T.   0402
Vaughan, Curtis   0575
Venter, C. J. H.   0642
Verner, D. C.   0714
Viard, A.   0273, 0399
Vine, W. E.   0909
Viviano, Benedict T.   0006
von, Adolf   0456
von Campenhausen, Hans   0580
von Lips, H.   0169, 0256

von Schlatter, Adolf   0897
Wainwright, Geoffrey   0029, 0407, 0659, 0681, 0737
Wainwright, John J.   0499, 0852
Wanke, Joachim   0607
Ward, Ronald A.   0919
Warren, Max   0578
Warth, Walter   0896
Wegenast, K.   0579
Weiser, Alfons   0496, 0550, 0564, 0677, 0715
Weiss, Bernhard   0086
Wells, P.   0118, 0242
Wendland, H.-D.   0488
Westerholm, Stephen   0003, 0662, 0829
Westphal, Carol J.   0059, 0787
White, John L.   0627
White, N. J. D.   0875
White, Robert A.   0269
Wiebe, Ben   0085, 0807
Wiederkehr, D.   0245, 0276
Wilhelm-Hooijebergh, A. E.   0285
Willmington, Harold L.   0182, 0299, 0332, 0358, 0522
Wilshire, Leland E.   0092, 0094, 0845, 0853
Wilson, J. P.   0314
Wilson, S. G.   0606
Windisch, Hans   0432
Winter, Bruce W.   0197, 0784
Wintle, B. C.   0158
Wohlenberg, Gustav   0871, 0874
Wolfe, B. Paul   0531, 0702, 0704
Wolter, Michael   0021, 0639
Wright, David F.   0013, 0183, 0266, 0425, 0543, 0664, 0842
Wuest, Kenneth S.   0893
Wulf, F.   0305, 0403
Yarbrough, Robert W.   0075
Young, Frances   0565, 0645
Young, Jerry R.   0025, 0184, 0373, 0390

Ziesler, John A.   0640
Zmijewski, Josef   0614
Zorn, Raymond O.   0346